Dresden
P L A T E

M000200768

New Quilts from an Old Favorite

American Quilter's Society

P. O. Box 3290 • Paducah, KY 42002-3290

www.americanquilter.com

Sponsors

Thanks to the following sponsors:

Fairfield
Quality Polyester Products for Home and Industry

JANOME
Because You Simply Love To Sew™

Clover

EDITORS: BARBARA SMITH & SHELLEY HAWKINS
GRAPHIC DESIGN: LYNDA SMITH
COVER DESIGN: MICHAEL BUCKINGHAM
QUILT PHOTOGRAPHY: CHARLES R. LYNCH
(UNLESS OTHERWISE NOTED)

Library of Congress Cataloging-in-Publication Data
Dresden plates : new quilts from an old favorite / by American
Quilter's Society.
    p. cm.
    Summary: "The Dresden Plate quilt block is showcased in the annual
international challenge, New Quilts from an Old Favorite, sponsored
by The Museum of the American Quilter's Society. Seventeen Finalists
share their tips, techniques, and patterns"-- Provided by publisher.
    ISBN 1-57432-901-4
    1. Patchwork--Patterns. 2. Quilting--Patterns. 3. Patchwork quilts--
Competitions--United States. I. American Quilter's society.

TT835.D724 2006
746.46'041--dc22
            2006003162

Located in Paducah, Kentucky, the American Quilter's Society (AQS) is dedicated to promoting the accomplishments of today's quilters. Through its publications and events, AQS strives to honor today's quiltmakers and their work and to inspire future creativity and innovation in quiltmaking.

Additional copies of this book may be ordered from the American Quilter's Society, PO Box 3290, Paducah, KY 42002-3290, call toll-free 1-800-626-5420, or online at www.AmericanQuilter.com.

Copyright © 2006, American Quilter's Society

All rights reserved. No part of this book may be reproduced, stored in any retrieval system, or transmitted in any form, or by any means including but not limited to electronic, mechanical, photocopy, recording, or otherwise, without the written consent of the author and publisher. Patterns may be copied for personal use only.

Proudly printed and bound in the
United States of America

The Museum of the American Quilter's Society has created this contest to recognize and share with others the fascinating variety of interpretations that quilters bring forth from a single traditional quilt pattern. This book is dedicated to all those who see a traditional quilt block and can visualize both its link to the past and its bridge to the future.

The Museum of the American Quilter's Society (MAQS)

MAQS is an exciting place where the public can learn more about quilts, quiltmaking, and quiltmakers, and experience quilts that inspire and delight.

MAQS seeks to celebrate today's quilts and quiltmakers through exhibits of quilts from the MAQS collection and selected temporary exhibits. By providing a variety of workshops and other programs, MAQS helps to encourage, inspire, and enhance the development of today's quilter.

Whether presenting new or antique quilts, MAQS promotes understanding of and respect for all quilts – new and antique, traditional and innovative, machine made and handmade, utility and art.

Contents

Preface

While preservation of the past is a museum's primary function, its greatest service is performed as it links the past to the present and to the future. With that intention, the Museum of the American Quilter's Society (MAQS) sponsors an annual contest and exhibit called New Quilts from an Old Favorite.

Created to acknowledge our quiltmaking heritage and to recognize innovation, creativity, and excellence, the contest challenges today's quiltmakers to interpret a single traditional quilt block in a work of their own design. Each year contestants respond with a myriad of stunning interpretations.

Dresden Plate: New Quilts from an Old Favorite is a wonderful representation of these interpretations. In this book you'll find a brief description of the 2006 contest, followed by a presentation of the five award winners and the 13 finalists and their quilts.

Full-color photographs of the quilts accompany each quiltmaker's comments – comments that provide insight into their widely diverse creative processes. Full-size templates for the traditional Dresden Plate block are included to form the basis for your own rendition. Tips, techniques, and patterns contributed by the contest winners offer an artistic framework for your own work.

Our wish is that *Dresden Plate: New Quilts from an Old Favorite* will further our quiltmaking heritage as new quilts based on the Dresden Plate block are inspired by the outstanding quilts, patterns, and instructions in this book.

The Contest

Although the contest encouraged unconventional creativity, there were some basic requirements for entries:

- Quilts entered in the contest were to be recognizable in some way as being related to the Dresden Plate block.
- The finished size of the quilt was to be a minimum of 50" in width and height but could not exceed 80" in any one dimension.
- Quilting was required on each quilt entered in the contest.
- A quilt could be entered only by the person(s) who made it.
- Each entry must have been completed after December 31, 2002.

To enter the contest, each quiltmaker was asked to submit an entry form and two slides of their quilt – one of the full quilt, and a second of a detail from the piece. In the Dresden Plate contest, quiltmakers from around the world responded to the challenge.

Three jurors viewed dozens of slides, deliberating over design, use of materials, interpretation of the theme, and technical excellence. Eventually they narrowed the field of entries to 18 finalists who were invited to submit their quilts for judging.

With quilts by the 18 finalists assembled, three judges meticulously examined the pieces, evaluating them again for design, innovation, theme, and workmanship. First- through fifth-place award winners were selected and notified.

Each year the New Quilts from an Old Favorite contest winners and finalists are featured in an exhibit that opens at the Museum of the American Quilter's Society in Paducah, Kentucky. Over a two-year period, the exhibit travels to a number of museums across North America and is viewed by thousands of quilt enthusiasts. Corporate sponsorship of the contest helps to underwrite costs, enabling even smaller museums across the country to display the exhibit.

Annually, the contest winners and finalists are included in a beautiful book published by the American Quilter's Society. *Dresden Plate: New Quilts from an Old Favorite* is the thirteenth in the contest, exhibit, and publication series. It joins the following other traditional block designs used as contest themes: Double Wedding Ring, Log Cabin, Kaleidoscope, Mariner's Compass, Ohio Star, Pineapple, Storm at Sea, Bear's Paw, Tumbling Blocks, Feathered Star, Monkey Wrench, and Seven Sisters.

For information about entering the current year's New Quilts from an Old Favorite contest, write to Museum of the American Quilter's Society at PO Box 1540, Paducah, KY, 42002-1540; call (270) 442-8856; or visit MAQS online at www.quiltmuseum.org.

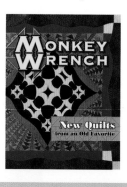
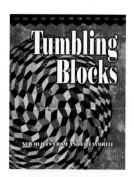

The Dresden Plate block represents a coming together of fabric, economics, and marketing. In 1906, The Ladies Art Company catalog offered pattern #408, titled Chrysthanthemum. The construction of this block is identical to the Dresden Plate blocks marketed during the 1930s by Ruby McKim, *Prairie Farmer, Wallaces' Farmer,* Home Art Studios, and *Successful Farming*. As seen in Barbara Brackman's *Encyclopedia of Appliqué*, the blocks feature a circle of blades with rounded tips. The pointed tips of the similar Aster and China Aster blocks published during this period echo the earlier fan motifs of crazy quilts from the late nineteenth century.

After the end of World War I in 1918, American dye manufacturers began using colors developed during the war. Prior to this, Germany provided most of the world's dyestuff. The war prevented United States' manufacturers from using these dyes, so American firms developed their own. Additionally, patented German dye formulas were made available as part of war reparations. The American fabric industry bounced back, producing inexpensive cotton prints in the bright pastels we have seen in quilts made during this time.

The Black Thursday stock market crash of October 24, 1929, ushered in the Great Depression. Printed feedsacks became a marketing tool for flour and sugar companies, enticing quilters with their bright, lively colors. In this arena of economy, Dresden Plate, Grandmother's Flower Garden, and Double Wedding Ring became the defining quilt patterns of the time. Newspapers and magazines printed quilt block patterns to encourage readership, often printing a series over several months. Quilt designers began marketing themselves and their patterns, as well as quilt kits.

Today's quilters, with unprecedented disposable income and leisure time, take full advantage of the incredible range of fabric available to them to create the quilts you see here. They have used the marketing tools of the Internet and the design assistance of computers to bring their ideas to life. Their imaginative designs and techniques will inspire you to create your own interpretation of this diverse block. The Dresden Plate block may be an old favorite, but it has become entirely new through the vision of today's quilters.

Judy Schwender
Curator of Collections and Registrar,
Museum of the American Quilter's Society

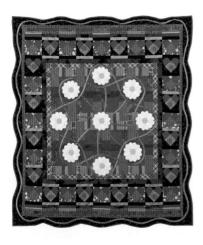

Cathy Pilcher Sperry

Cincinnati, Ohio

My mother's passion for sewing rubbed off on me quite early in life, and has grown through the years. My earliest memory of Mom is seeing her at the sewing machine creating beautiful clothes. When I was 11, she bought me flannel fabric and a gown pattern, which I made in several days and asked for more fabric. From that point, I made most of my clothes.

I was very active in 4-H and sewing contests in high school. I graduated from Oregon State University with a degree in home economics education, and taught junior and senior high school for eight years. Beginning as a dressmaker and sewing in clothing competitions, I was aware of accuracy and attention to detail.

After moving across the country to New Jersey in 1985 with my husband, I was 3,000 miles from home and lonely. The Newcomer's Club delivered its newsletter, which advertised a quilting group it sponsored. My grandmother quilted, but I didn't know much about it. I really just wanted to join the group to meet new friends. These friendships have enriched my life. We've lived all over the country and I always find the nicest quilters in each new place. Quilting is now something I share with my mother and daughter. It is my lifeline. With all our relocations, quilting has been a stabilizing force.

Fortunately, I was able to stay home and raise our daughter and son. By managing my time well, quilting fit into my daily schedule. Now that the kids are in college, I can spend eight to 12 hours a day designing and quilting. Laundry is done while I'm cutting templates, and dinner is prepared when it's time to take a break from quilting. I also exercise daily, and that time is spent thinking about designs or problem-solving with a particular project. Ideas come at the most unexpected times, and I try to be prepared with a sketch pad and camera.

I present quilt programs to church and community groups, and try to design and make at least two auction quilts annually for charity. Last year, I completed four quilts for competitions. I love detail and enjoy embellishing quilts. It is very gratifying to have people view my quilts and find surprises in the details such as beading, bobbin writing, and special binding treatments.

Inspiration and Design

Inspiration is all around me: in the church sanctuary, in nature, in architecture, in literature, and from my family. I try to imagine how everything can be used in a quilt design. When I began quilting, I would play with the bolts of fabric at the store. With the bolts stacked neatly together, the color scheme for an entire quilt could be designed. Most times, the fabrics were never purchased, but it was a good exercise for gaining color confidence.

The Dresden Plate was the design of the first quilt that was passed down to me from my grandmother. This quilt reminds me of daisies, so when I found the daisy batik fabric, it all came together. Journal ideas were kept from several classes I took in Paducah, so I returned to this journal while

Cathy's photo by Amanda Hovillion

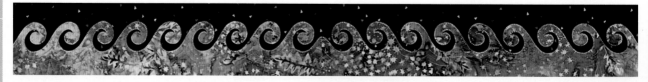

CAN YOU FEEL THE SPIRIT?

56½" x 57"

"I believe the frame around the quilt and the extra pizzazz added by embellishments make an ordinary quilt an extraordinary piece of art."

designing. I started with three different designs, decided on the placement of each, and then drew in the bands of Flying Geese. Many different techniques were incorporated in this quilt, as well as embellishments. Freezer paper and plastic templates, machine and hand appliqué, machine paper piecing, machine quilting, bobbin writing, hand beading, and piped binding were used.

Hand beading

It's always a challenge to put together a piecing plan with a design like this. After analyzing the design, I write a sequence of steps. This is an invaluable tool for the many interruptions I have during the day. The steps for this quilt are as follows:

1. Piece the background areas.
2. Prepare and piece pink, green, and aqua Dresden Plates.
3. Foundation piece the Flying Geese sections.
4. Piece Flying Geese sections into the background.
5. Hand appliqué the green Dresden Plate to the pink one.
6. Hand appliqué the Dresden Plate unit to the background.
7. Hand appliqué the aqua Dresden Plate to the background.
8. Piece the checkerboard border and add it to the quilt top.
9. Machine appliqué the wave design to the outer border.
10. Machine appliqué the corner pieces.
11. Piece the outer borders to the quilt top.

The biggest challenge came with quilting the daisy background. I quilted all the major areas in the ditch first with metallic thread. Then, the daisies were quilted with variegated trilobal polyester thread. The quilting was so heavy and dense that it became a problem to keep the quilt flat. I considered removing the machine quilting, but it added so much dimension that I had to keep going and just deal with it. The quilt had to be blocked to the floor several times before and after it was bound to minimize distortion at the edges.

CAN YOU FEEL THE SPIRIT? is the result of deciding that the worst possible thing that could happen is that the project might end up in the trash. Once I really believed this, I was set free. My quilts aren't always designed before they are sewn, but my designs have begun to flow more freely and my quilts are now much more spontaneous. One needs to take the risk to try new things, experiment, and not be afraid to fail.

Creating Value Contrast and Dimension

The contrast of value is the most important element of this design, particularly in the large green Dresden Plate. A collection of values was selected to create dimension. There is often just a slight difference between a light medium and medium light, but it is enough to create the illusion of depth and movement. Of course, value is relative and it all depends on what is next to it. By using soft contrasts next to each other on the pink Dresden Plate, the stronger green, more vibrant contrasts are allowed to pop and create a dimensional look.

Making plastic templates for each blade piece allowed me to cut each fabric piece individually and control the placement of the printed designs. One set of each blade was cut, then placed on the design wall to check value placement before cutting the entire block. The value contrast is key to this quilt, but selecting fabrics that are different in printed texture also added to the visual success.

There are two different blades in the green block (pages 12 and 13). Five pieces of each blade were prepared, and only half of the fifth blade was used. After each half blade was pieced and joined in the center, folding along the center seam and stitching across the top created the point. When turned right side out, the point was ready for hand appliqué. Each blade was finished before joining them all in the block, which was pieced by machine. It was hand appliquéd to the

pink Dresden Plate, then the combined plates were hand appliquéd as one unit to the background.

Additional texture was created on the green Dresden Plate with machine quilting. Each template area has a different design. More detail was used on the plain fabrics. The thread color was changed with each value, allowing the quilting to enhance the total design. I used the extra blades along with the exact batting and backing in the quilt for samples. This helped me get my machine settings perfect and make note of them in my journal for reference during the project.

Taking pictures with my digital camera throughout the process helped me critique. I could add and subtract different elements and compare them on the computer screen while it was still possible to make changes. Once my design colors were in place, I took a picture and printed it out in black and white (fig. 1). If the depth, dimension, and movement still exist, I know I'm on the right track.

Fig. 1. A black-and-white printed photo helps to show contrast in value.

Green and pink Dresden Plate block

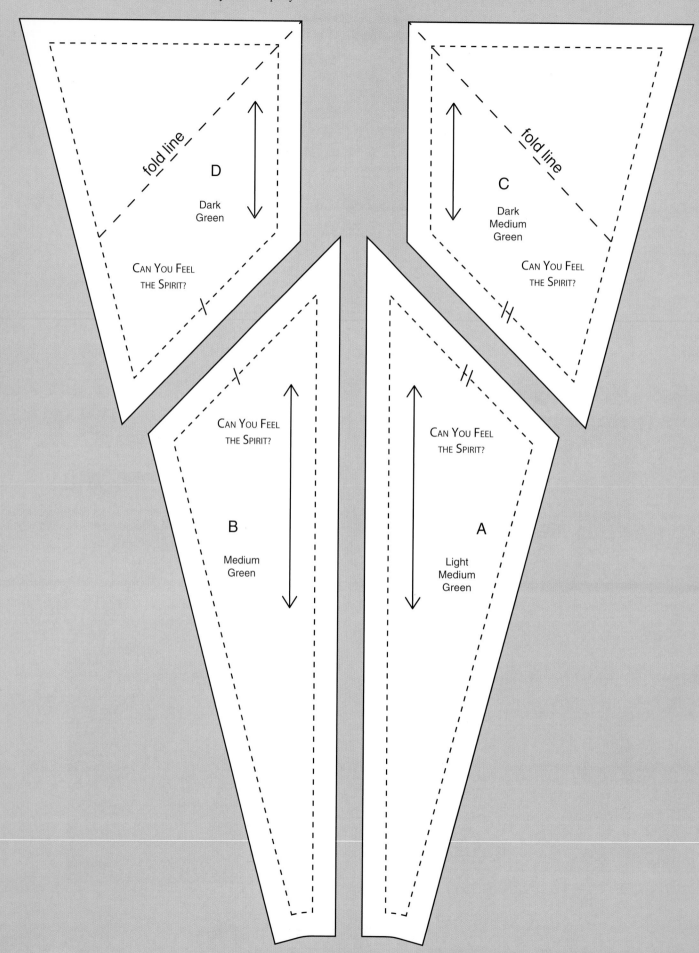

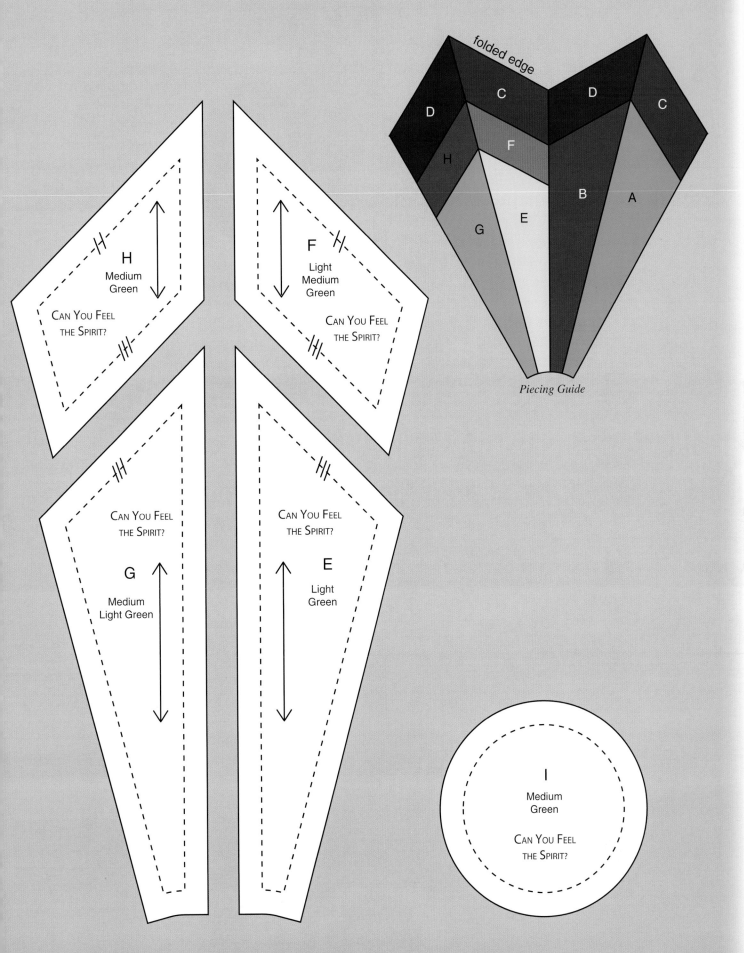

folded edge

D C D C

F

H

B

G E A

Piecing Guide

H
Medium
Green

CAN YOU FEEL
THE SPIRIT?

F
Light
Medium
Green

CAN YOU FEEL
THE SPIRIT?

CAN YOU FEEL
THE SPIRIT?

G
Medium
Light Green

CAN YOU FEEL
THE SPIRIT?

E
Light
Green

I
Medium
Green

CAN YOU FEEL
THE SPIRIT?

Second Place

Sherri Bain Driver

Tucson, Arizona

I was fortunate to grow up in a family that valued creativity and fun. My mother was a wonderful seamstress who rarely followed patterns. Instead, she modified them, switching sleeves or collars and adding her own design elements.

My dad was a mechanical engineer and loved to invent in his spare time. As a kid, he made toys from stuff around the house. Dad's workshop was in the basement and he always had fascinating projects in progress. Because he felt our elementary school carnival had only predictable games and nothing for older kids, he invented and built a game for our school. I grew up thinking everybody's dad created carnival games in their basement.

Raised in this climate, I was encouraged to try just about anything. I was always busy making something – cardboard doll houses, sequined holiday ornaments, or braided halters for toy horses. My parents were enthusiastic supporters of my creative efforts. Mom taught me to sew when I was eight, and I made most of my clothes for many years. Mom understood that some projects just don't work out and should be abandoned rather than allowing them to consume more time. That explains my lack of guilt over the unfinished objects in my sewing room today.

My first quilting class began with a lesson in drafting blocks on graph paper. I've always appreciated that approach because it gave me a firm under-standing of the basics. After learning the fundamentals, I began to design my own quilts, doodling blocks and settings on graph paper.

I have a beautiful sketchbook that contains alternating graph paper and blank sheets. At first I used only the graph paper and focused on traditional quilts. Eventually, I used the blank pages and found my creativity expanding by drawing without the constraints of straight lines. Today, doodling is still a method of design for me. While on long drives with my husband, I bring my sketchbook and am lucky to be able to draw for many miles without getting carsick.

I look to many non-quilt items for design inspiration. I have an inspiration file that holds clipped pictures, doodles, and other beautiful or interesting things. I dip into that file often to spice up an idea or to look for solutions to design problems.

Inspiration and Design

My initial idea was to enlarge the Dresden Plate block and divide the wedges into smaller shapes. I sketched out a few ideas, but soon realized that fabric choices needed to be made so I could plan shapes to complement fabric motifs. From my stash, I chose ikats, stripes, and plaids in a narrow range of earthy colors, including blacks, browns, grays, and off-whites. The colors were reminiscent of Native American pottery and baskets. Too many fabrics were chosen for just one Dresden Plate, so I toyed with the idea of making more blocks.

Sherri's photo by Briana Ford, Glamour Shots

REINVENTING THE WHEEL
65" x 65"

"The love of fabric, pattern, shapes, and color attracted me to quilting. As I became more involved, I discovered an added bonus of the wonderful community of quilters."

The idea of overlapping four Dresden Plates came from the traditional Card Trick block. I was always fascinated with the way the cards appear to be entwined. Wondering if the same effect would happen with other shapes, I traced round coasters in the same entwined configuration and was very pleased with the result (fig. 1).

Fig. 1. Tracing around coasters to make the circles helped this original drawing take shape.

Then, I traced a 22½-degree commercial template onto see-through plastic and placed the plastic over fabrics to audition motifs. Once motifs were isolated, I drew lines on the plastic to indicate seam lines, and then made a separate template for each piece in the wedge. The section at the narrow end of the wedge was too skinny for extra piecing, so I planned to fussy cut patterned fabric. For the widest part of the wedge, I could use large-patterned fabric or plan a pieced section. The middle section and the wide end became foundation- or strip-piecing areas.

I looked to many sources for inspiration. I have several Dover books of copyright-free designs. My favorite is a book with designs from all over the world, which has a section on circular designs including motifs from Egypt, Greece, and ancient civilizations. Other objects of inspiration included hubcaps, which were adapted for my quilt.

Dresden Plate Construction

The following instructions are for constructing one of the blocks in this quilt. Yardage requirements depend on the number of motif repeats per yard.

1. Using see-through template plastic, draw templates for pieces A, B, and D (pages 18 and 19). Make small holes in the templates where indicated to mark pivot points for setting in pieces. Cut 16 fabric pieces of each template, fussy cutting exact repeats if you wish. Mark the pivot points on the pieces.

2. Piece C is a two-section foundation. Make 16 copies of each section. Following numerical order, foundation piece the sections. Trim excess paper and fabric along the outside line. Join sections 1 and 2. Press the seam allowances open.

3. Join pieces A, B, and C to make a wedge, setting the points of A and C into B. To do this, clip the B pieces one or two threads from the marked pivot point. With the pieces right sides together and B underneath, align the edges for the first portion of the seam. Sew from the outer edge to the pivot point and stop with the needle down. Raise the presser foot and realign the edges for the rest of the seam. A pair of tweezers is handy for this. Complete the seam. Repeat to make all the wedges. Remove the foundation paper.

4. Join the wedges, leaving the seam allowances free on the outer edge so you can set in the D pieces. Press the seam allowances open. If your Dresden Plate doesn't lie flat, make small adjustments in the seams.

5. Set in the D pieces around the edges. To cover the hole in the center, prepare a circle with a finished 2¾" diameter and appliqué it over the hole.

To make a quilt like mine, you'll need four blocks. You can make the same block, or be creative and design your own. To do this, make a template of a single unpieced wedge by tracing a wedge from your completed block. Now divide the wedge into new shapes, adding seam allowances where needed.

When the four plates were finished, I pinned each one to a large piece of paper to avoid distortion in the next steps. Then I sewed 1½" wide double-fold bias strips around most of the perimeter of each block.

Once the four blocks were arranged and overlapped, they were basted together to form a single unit. I machine basted just inside the bias strip, using water-soluble thread. Then I carefully tore away the paper and trimmed the excess fabric underneath.

Because the unit of Dresden Plates was so large, I made a background with a hole in the middle to save fabric. The background was taped to my kitchen floor to avoid distortion, then I pinned the Dresden Plate unit to the center and basted it with water-soluble thread. Excess fabric behind the unit was trimmed, leaving a ¼" seam allowance.

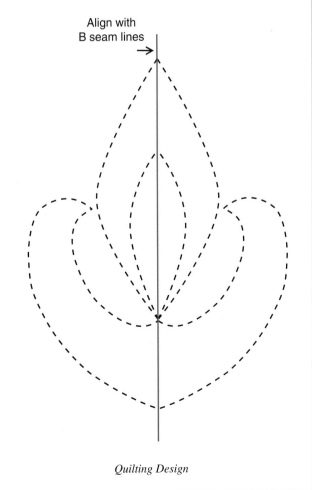

Align with
B seam lines →

Quilting Design

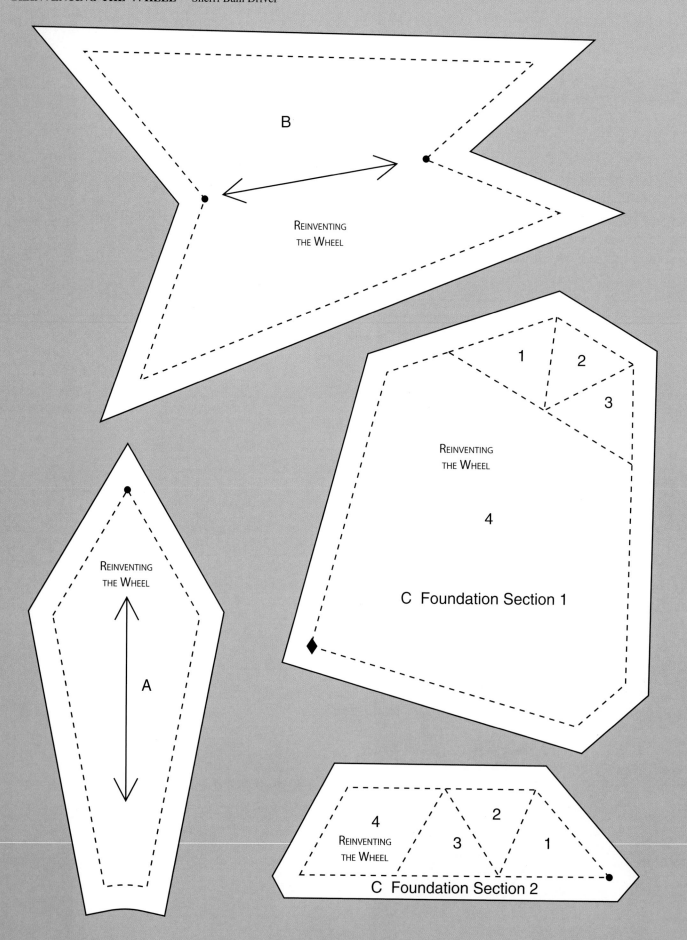

B

REINVENTING
THE WHEEL

1   2

3

REINVENTING
THE WHEEL

4

C Foundation Section 1

REINVENTING
THE WHEEL

A

4   2

REINVENTING   3   1
THE WHEEL

C Foundation Section 2

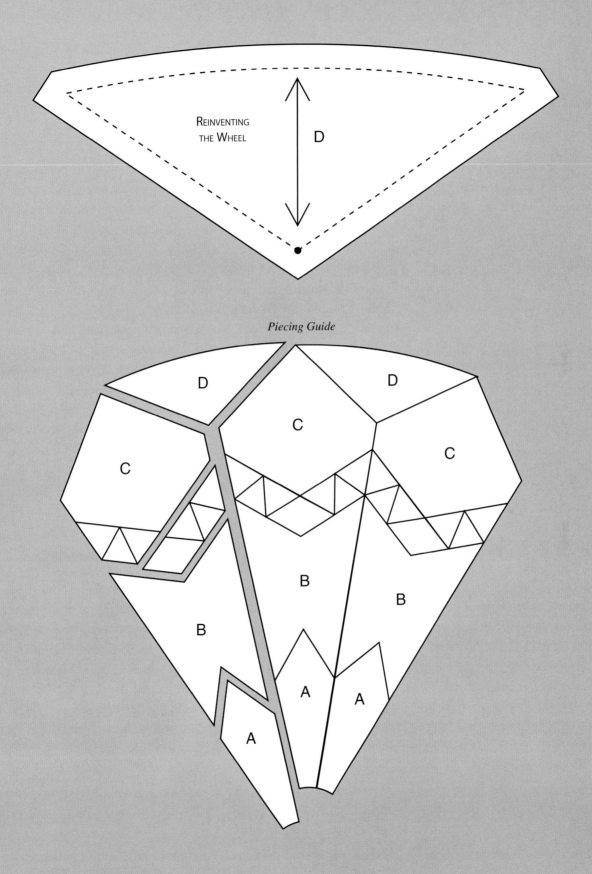

REINVENTING
THE WHEEL

D

Piecing Guide

Third Place

Nadine Ruggles

Gerlingen, Germany

After making quilts for 15 years, I still can't get enough. There are so many quilts I want to make, new tools and techniques to try, and fabric to buy, that I probably won't live long enough to do it all. I try to fit quilting into my life every day. It is higher on my priority list than eating! My family is very supportive of my obsession, and they know quilting is a great stress reliever for me.

Most of my current pieces are original designs. Some of my work is traditional, and some is more innovative. I really enjoy the challenge of designing my own patterns, combining traditional designs in new ways, and working on design challenges as the quilt is constructed. I love to determine what can be done to a pattern or block to make something new and individual.

Recently, I've been plowing through the mountain of unfinished objects (UFOs) that have amassed over the years. In the beginning, there were just so many quilts I wanted to make and ideas to try, projects were left unfinished before moving on to the next one. There are still a lot of quilts and ideas, but I have more self-control now. I try to finish one UFO a month and not start new projects lightly. Some projects can be finished and donated, others used in my home or given to friends and family, and still others are made over into something totally different.

There are some projects I've had to let go permanently because they have been around so long that I don't like them anymore, or there were design problems that were insurmountable. I used to feel guilty about that, but if you don't enjoy making it, why do it? Quilting is supposed to be fun, and besides that, I've learned something from the unfinished projects, even if it's what not to do next time. Now if I can only let go of my bags and bags of tiny scraps.

Inspiration and Design

The best thing about this quilt is its humble beginning as leftovers from two other projects. I began thinking about the Dresden Plate contest shortly after finishing my quilt for the previous year's Seven Sisters contest. I jotted many ideas on paper, and discarded most of them just as quickly as they were written. After spending some time cleaning out my studio and digging through my UFOs and remainders, I came across the pieces for two round medallions made with a 9-degree wedge ruler. There they were, saying "we could be your Dresden Plate quilt!"

I thought a Dresden Plate that was somewhat "bargello-ish" would be wonderful, so the wide end of each plate petal was rounded before they were sewn together. At that point, just two plates wouldn't do, so I chose slightly different fabrics and made two more plates. The plates were hand appliquéd to the black background with silk thread. The appliqué was a bit difficult due to the horizontal seams that sometimes fell right at the edge of the petals and had to be turned under, bulky seam allowances and all.

The partial chain of squares border was also made up of leftover bits from another quilt. The

PAISLEY PAVANE

58½" x 58½"

"Over 3,000 hot-fix crystals in different colors were added to the finished quilt. Maybe it should have been called The Bling Quilt, but PAISLEY PAVANE sounded more fitting for an elegant quilt."

blocks were assembled in an off-center setting, and the borders added. I first thought about using feather quilting designs, but because I planned to add crystal embellishments, paisley designs were used to provide more logical areas for the "crystal icing."

Paisley quilting designs with crystals

PAISLEY PAVANE was quilted with many different cotton and rayon variegated threads in shades of green, rose, and burgundy. The plate centers were quilted with small paisley designs, which are not visible from the front of the finished quilt. The quilt was washed, blocked, and bound before the plate centers were applied.

I made four different embroidered centers for the plates. Each circle was embroidered with rayon thread on cotton fabric over a layer of batting and tear-away stabilizer. Batting adds even more stabilization, as well as extra dimension to heavily embroidered designs. The circles were trimmed to size, sewn, and flipped pillow-style to make the appliqué easier. The embroidered circles were appliquéd over the quilting in the plate centers, so that the quilting inside the centers only shows on the quilt back.

A Modern Mode of Transfer

Transferring quilting designs is quite possibly the bane of my existence. It's not my least favorite part of quilting (that would have to be basting!), but it runs a very close second. There is no one true way that works best for every quilt or every design when it comes to marking. I've tried a few different methods of marking on dark fabrics when I didn't have a stencil or the designs were too complex to make one, and the following method works best:

Draw or trace your quilting design on white paper. The lines on the drawing need to be very clear, and I've found that a black felt-tip marker with a very fine tip works much better than a pencil, which is usually too light (fig. 1). With a computer scanner and a graphics program, import your quilting design. Experiment with the settings on the scanner software to get the best import, with 150 dots per inch or more, and darken or lighten the image to get the best contrast. The image needs to be clearly black and white, without shades of gray. If there are any stray marks, use the eraser in the graphics program to delete them. A graphics tablet – which is an input device like a mouse, except it's a pen and tablet – will give you better control when editing.

Fig. 1. *Import your design on the computer.*

When the image is clean and clear, select the whole image and use the "invert" command to change the drawing to white lines on a black background (fig. 2). Print the drawing on thin white paper. With a light box, you'll be able to clearly see the light shining through the white lines on the paper, and transfer your design to black or dark fabrics. A fine, white marking pen works well for this technique. Choose one that is clearly visible, doesn't rub away completely before it's quilted, and washes out completely. Always test it on your fabric before use.

Fig. 2. Invert the design to white lines on a black background.

If a quilting design is too large to fit on standard paper, divide it into small sections and use registration marks to fit it back together for marking the quilt. You can also take the design to a copy shop and reduce it to fit standard computer paper, invert the design as described, then return to the copy shop and have it enlarged to the proper size. The copy shop could possibly invert the design in its original size to save a few steps.

Fourth Place

Julia Graber

Brooksville, Mississippi

Working at The Clothes Line, my parent's fabric store, in my early twenties sparked my interest in quiltmaking. One of my first attempts at this craft was making two very heavy woolen comforters that were pieced and tied. I sold one at the store and kept the other, which I still enjoy to this day.

After teaching school for three years, I married Paul Graber, and we have reared five boys and one girl. We also raise hogs, catfish, corn, and soybeans, and are involved in church activities and mission work in Romania. Even though we're busy, I've found that it's like the saying goes: "You have time to do what you want to do." So I make time for sewing and quilting. I treasure my family's interest and comments about my quilts and think they enjoy my enthusiasm.

Most of the quilts I make are the service type, especially for charity. In recent years, I've enjoyed making more of the creative art quilts, receiving a lot of inspiration from quilt shows, books, and magazines. My knowledge of tips and techniques comes simply from reading.

I come from a large family, and in recent years, four generations of the women get together for a week to ten days to sew, quilt, make baskets, talk, and laugh. Two of my sisters, Barbara Cline and Polly Yoder, are also finalists in this contest. It was great fun to share our joys and frustrations with each other and watch our unique quilts come together.

Inspiration and Design

The Dresden Plate pattern struck me as something that I could make come alive. Having been a finalist in the Seven Sisters contest gave me the courage to try again.

This pattern evoked fond memories of a 1950s' quilt that was on my bed when I was a teenager. Approximately 12 or 18 of the traditional blocks were appliquéd to the background squares with a hand-sewn buttonhole stitch. This quilt was given to my parents from my maternal grandmother. Even though I loved that quilt, I knew this was not the type of quilt I wanted to make.

I wanted a big medallion plate to focus on in the center of my quilt. Trying to think of another block that represents food to put on the plate, I considered the Pickle Dish and the Pineapple. I pieced square Pineapple blocks, and then cut out the blades of the Dresden Plate from those blocks.

I enjoy bright, bold colors and chose purple to complement gold. To create interest, the color values graduated in the Pineapple from light to dark, then back to light. The blocks were paper pieced, making this my first major attempt at this method. I expected paper piecing to be difficult and a waste of fabric, but soon learned otherwise with a little practice. I learned to enjoy the sewing, pressing, flipping, and trimming that resulted in precise blocks. Picking the paper off the back was relaxing work during quiet evenings of visiting with my husband and children in the living room.

Julia's photo by Amy J. Graber, Amy's Photography

A PLATE OF PINEAPPLES

58" x 58"

"In looking at A PLATE OF PINEAPPLES, I'm amazed at how my eyes dart around the quilt, even though I'm looking at the same image or segment of the plate on either side."

I made individual blocks, sewed them together, and then cut the blade from those blocks. It was a challenge to choose the background color for the Dresden Plate. A few unfinished blades were auditioned on different fabrics (fig. 1). After deciding on orange, I laid the finished block on the background and added different borders and took pictures of them to see which combination I liked the best (fig. 2).

These pictures were e-mailed to my family to get their opinions. Most of the young people pre-

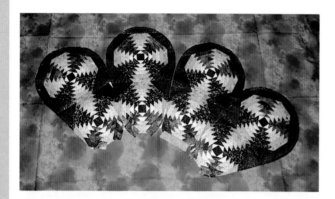

Fig. 2. The design was then auditioned with two different borders.

ferred the orange background with the striped border because it had pizzazz. A few of my sisters liked the yellow background more. I struggled myself, but felt the striped border was too busy and detracted from the main design. Also, there were no orange or striped fabrics in the Dresden Plate, so I chose the yellow background.

Fig. 1. Unfinished blades were auditioned on different fabrics.

Pineapple to Dresden Plate

My first step in construction was to find the basic Pineapple block, which I got from a previous *New Quilts from an Old Favorite* contest book. After enlarging, I photocopied many blocks and sewed only two blocks together by machine (fig. 3).

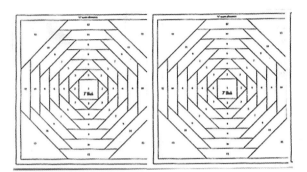

Fig. 3. *Two Pineapple blocks were joined as a base for the Dresden Plate blade.*

A challenge arose when I realized the whole Dresden Plate blade could not be pieced from those two blocks to get the desired size. In retrospect, I should have sewn three together because parts of the third block had to be added later. On freezer paper, a blade was drawn with a 30-degree angle on one end and a curve on the opposite end that was drawn with a round lid. The template was placed on the blocks and the Dresden Plate blade was cut out (fig. 4).

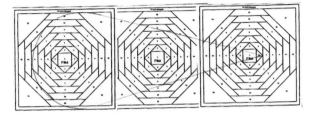

Fig. 4. *Dresden Plate blade template placed on joined blocks*

After sewing all the blades together, I hand appliquéd the Dresden Plate to the background, then hand appliquéd the center circle. Each strip of the Pineapple was machine quilted with cursive *e's* and *l's*, using metallic gold thread. Rayon and other threads were also used in the quilting around the plate and background.

Cursive e's *and* l's *were quilted in strips of the Pineapples.*

Polly Yoder

Greenwood, Delaware

I have six sisters and we share an inherited love for any kind of sewing, mutually stimulating creativity, and warm times together. Our parents owned a dry goods/sewing machine store, and most of us were a part of its ongoing operation. Though I'm sure none of us was aware just how rich this exposure was, it has proven to be an invaluable asset to us over the years.

My parents both have been gifted with artistic ability. They always encouraged us to try anything in which we were interested. Being surrounded by the pursuit of beauty and being encouraged to express what was within our own souls has much to do with the way we siblings have enjoyed working with our hands to create things of beauty.

My grandmother was an unusually gifted woman. While in high school, I put my very first stitches in a quilt at her house. After being invited to quilt for the evening, I worked hard for hours and accomplished about five or six inches. I've often wondered if Grandmother took those stitches out, but she was very affirming!

That evening began a wonderful love of quilting for me. Growing older, I realize how she has influenced me in my sewing and quilting. She made a wonderful

velvet comfort for my wedding present. Today, I am making my second velvet comfort, tucking them away for my grandchildren's wedding presents.

I feel the connection of the generations running through the fingers of my grandmother, mother, sisters, daughters, daughters-in-law, and now granddaughters. It's an invisible thread, made of many things, but mostly love, that draws us up and pulls us together. It is a connection to those who went before me, those with whom I share my life, and those who are yet to come. How very much I want to pass this on!

Sewing is the most relaxing thing I can do. Whether it is in my own cozy nook, at our church's sewing circle where we quilt and knot comforts for the less fortunate, or helping someone with a sewing problem, I find sewing, particularly quilting, to be an outlet for my creative energy. It is also a way to contribute to the lives of others.

My husband is an associate pastor of a Mennonite church and also owns a nursing home. We are the parents of six children. I often find my heart and hands busy at the things that are necessary for everyday living. But come the quiet evenings, or a snatched moment alone during the day, you will probably find me in my sewing room busy with the next project on my agenda and pondering the exciting possibilities for the future.

Polly's photo by Christine H. Miller

THE DAZZLING DRESDEN DOODLE
66½" x 54"

"It is such a compelling inspiration to look at the long line of women who sewed, quilted, and mended out of necessity. How blessed we are today to be held together by a love for the art, an appreciation for the finished work, and an excitement for quilts yet undreamed."

Dresden Plates wrapped around a curve

Inspiration and Design

I often doodle ribbon designs on paper when talking on the phone or sitting idle. It gives me something to do with my hands while my mind may be otherwise occupied. I have done this since grade school.

When two of my sisters, Barbara Cline and Julia Graber, who were finalists in last year's contest, challenged me to enter a quilt in this year's contest, my interest was piqued. Their encouragement definitely inspired me to give it a try. The inspiration to find an idea that suited my personality caused me to explore many different avenues of expression.

I got busy and doodled different Dresden Plate ideas. Most were traditional plates with a different spin, but one was my regular doodle ribbon in which I drew all different kinds and styles of Dresden Plates on the ribbon. When my daughter saw what I was toying with, she said, "Mom, that's the one. Go for it!" That was the encouragement I needed to press on.

The challenges of this quilt seemed to never end. First, I had to figure out how to make the plates look real when wrapped around the curves. It was going to take shading and pattern adjusting to make it look three-dimensional. I had never done shading before, so I needed to experiment with materials that could bring the dimensional effect to life. Tulle netting was used for the shading.

The incredible challenge of this quilt, the sheer magnitude of possibilities, and necessary investment of time and experimentation really got me out of my comfort zone. It was so exciting to explore new avenues of quilting, try things I had not even thought about before, find media that worked to express what was in my mind's eye, and realize that this was something I could create. It was just such an exhilarating, energizing, and motivating experience for me.

Bringing a Doodle to Life

First, I cut 8½" x 11" pieces of paper in half lengthwise. After taping them together in a long strip, I drew all sizes and shapes of Dresden Plates from various books. Next, my paper ribbon was scrolled around on the kitchen counter in a pleasing design, and I took many pictures from all angles (fig. 1).

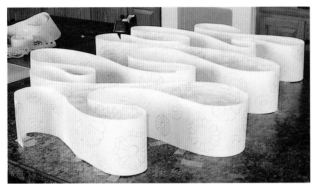

Fig. 1. *Strips of paper were taped together and then scrolled into a pleasing ribbon shape.*

I had a photocopy store enlarge the picture to 48" x 66". They made two copies. One was used as a master and pinned to my design wall and the other was cut into individual pieces for my pattern (fig. 2).

Fig. 2. *The enlarged photographs of the ribbon served as a master design and a pattern.*

The freezer paper and needle-turn techniques were used to appliqué each Dresden Plate onto the ribbon pieces. I machine appliquéd a few of the plates to the quilt, but outside of that, the whole quilt was hand pieced (fig. 3). I then machine quilted the quilt, which was a fairly new experience for me.

Fig. 3. *Polly pinned ribbon segments to the master pattern on her design wall.*

Barbara Cline

Bridgewater, Virginia

My sewing career began when I constructed a simple dress in the eighth grade. Since then, garment making has waned and quilt design and construction have become a passion for me.

As each day unfolds, it becomes a piece of the beautiful tapestry of my life, designed and woven by God. The woof and warp of my life include my husband and our five teenage children, who each make valuable contributions to my quilting. My husband is my faithful advisor and critic, whose fresh perspective often gives me balance when I am working too closely with a project. The boys tease me about my quilts, which encourages me. The capable help from my daughters' editing and grammar skills polishes the quilt patterns I design and sell.

My father, mother, brother, and six sisters are important threads in my life cloth as well. My love of fabric has been influenced by my mother's artistic flair and skill with color in her oil and china painting. My sisters challenge and inspire my quilting creativity. Two of my sisters, Julia Graber and Polly Yoder, won fourth and fifth place in this contest.

Inspiration and Design

The idea for DRESDEN FANFARE spawned from my quilt STAR TRICKS, in which striped stars spin around in a circle forming a larger star (fig. 1). I own a business called Delightful Piecing in which I create and sell patterns. Several patterns have become reality and many are still in the idea stage. After marketing STAR TRICKS, I learned about this contest and decided to use the same idea with the Dresden Plate pattern.

I played around with some different fabrics and made a few fans. One of these was made with a striped fabric, which I really liked. The stripe emphasized the zigzag and gave some depth that the other fans did not.

Fig. 1. STAR TRICKS, *designed by Barbara, was the basis of the* DRESDEN FANFARE *design.*

Barbara's photo by Rebecca Cline

DRESDEN FANFARE

79" x 79"

"Because a fan was decided on for each petal, I used dark and light shades to create a zigzag effect. Organdy overlay created shade for the dark side of the stripe."

Initially, I pieced strips of light fabrics together. This process was repeated with darker fabrics. Then, I placed my fan pattern over the strips of fabric and cut the fans, making sure the lines fell at the same place each time (fig. 2). Next, the fans were sewn together and a center circle was appliquéd in place.

The larger petals were formed as I appliquéd the zigzag plates. Each large petal was then accented with a very narrow strip around the outer edge. The large plate was topstitched onto the center background fabric.

The next challenge was creating the right pattern for the zigzag border around the large center design. I was not sure how to get the right angle for the pattern, so my husband came to the rescue. The first background fabric was then sewn to the large zigzag circle. This circle was hand appliquéd to the second background fabric. The colorful stripe and the same first center background fabric added the finishing touches to the outer border.

Using free-motion quilting, I had decided to include a minimal amount of quilting, but one thing led to another and the finished quilt is quite closely quilted. The center background was quilted in radiant lines from the plate to the zigzag. A circular design was quilted on the outer background.

The outer border displays a special quilting feature. Large diamonds were quilted in metallic thread with a straight stitch. The second large diamonds, which overlaid the first row, were quilted with a zigzag stitch.

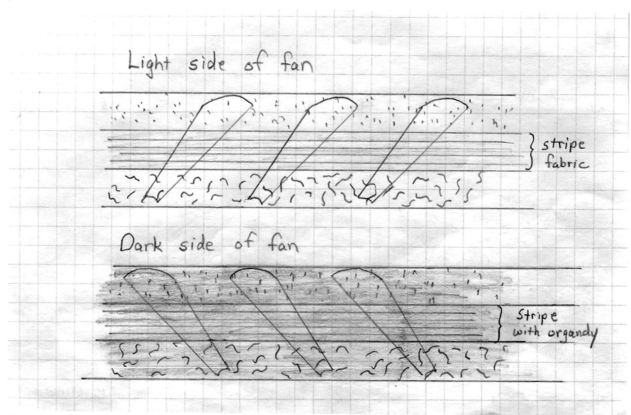

Fig. 2. *Sketch of the plan for cutting fans to achieve shading*

Quilting in the outer border features large diamonds in metallic thread.

Blades were carefully cut from light and dark pieced fabric strips to achieve a fan effect.

Piping and radiating quilting lines help define each blade of the large Dresden Plate.

Margo Ellis

Key West, Florida

My mom tells stories of me sitting at her feet as a three-year-old while she sewed. She kept me busy by letting me put pins in and out of a tomato pincushion. It must have been my first experience with pins and fabric. As I got older, I used my grandma's treadle machine to sew paper designs without thread in the needle.

My grandma often showed me the quilts she was planning to make. I inherited that trait with my boxes, bags, and stash of ready-to-make quilts. I have selected fabrics for a particular pattern and placed them together in a bag with the pattern. Needless to say, these bags often get raided when another idea emerges. You might say I'm a bag lady.

I enjoyed 4-H in school and learned to refine my clothes-making skills. I made several patchwork vests while in college, but didn't really start quilting in earnest until inheriting my grandmother's stash of unfinished patchwork pieces, clothes-making scraps, and sundry ribbons, rickrack, buttons, and bias tape.

My first quilt was a crazy patch of my grandma's scraps. It took me two years to finish because I didn't know the ins and outs of flip-and-sew piecing. Multiple layers often resulted because I had not worked from the inside out correctly. When I got divorced, it stayed with my ex. His girlfriend (we remained friends) brought it to me to see if it could be repaired. All that was left was the muslin interlining at that point.

In 1980, I was inspired to hand quilt by an appliquéd scene of hills and distant houses surrounded with a rainbow-striped border. Being self-taught, I thought the quilt had to be as tight in the hoop as embroidery. Try quilting with the fabric taut, and you know it is almost impossible to get more than four stitches to the inch.

The hoop with the quilt in it hung on the wall for two years before I finally finished the center. It ended up as a car trunk quilt until Hurricane Wilma flooded my car. Fortunately, we had no flooding or damage to our home, so my stash was safe.

I love to collect fabric and amass way more than needed. When I show non-quilters a new piece, I still don't have a good answer when they ask, "What are you going to use it for?" I usually just smile and shrug.

Margo's photo by Pat Hurt, Interstate Studio & Publishing Co.

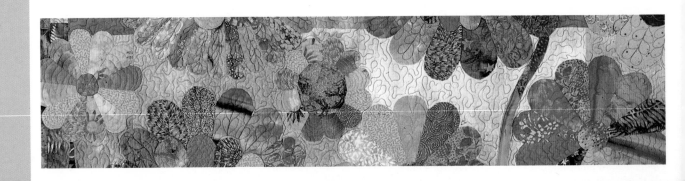

ROYAL POINCIANAS

64" x 64"

"The plates were hand pieced and assembled with what I call controlled randomness. I focused on color variations and envisioned orange blossoms surrounded by green leaves."

Inspiration and Design

From May to November, the royal poinciana trees around Key West bloom in every variation of red, yellow, and orange imaginable. It is easy to see why they are nicknamed flame trees. Each tree seems to flower on its own schedule and they peak at different times. Harbingers of summer in the tropics, the trees have been the inspiration for many artists.

Poinciana trees in full bloom

Walking my dogs every day under two royal poinciana trees that meet over the street, I have always wanted to make a quilt depicting them in full bloom. When the Dresden Plate was selected for the contest theme, I realized my inspiration could possibly find an outlet. Having recently treated myself to Electric Quilt™ 5 software, I began playing with ideas to demonstrate the flamboyance of the trees.

Now the hard part started. I seldom plan much in advance and just began collecting flame, leaf, and bark colors. I had a sizeable stash of oranges from previous quilts, but enjoyed finding more. I wanted the background to reflect the allure of the sky's interaction with the trees, so large rectangles of sky blues from hand-dying classes were used.

With a variety of sizes and types of plates, I began working on my design wall and almost gave up when they just didn't seem to work together. I needed a tree! I dug back into my bark colors and randomly assembled a vague tree shape. Once the tree was added, the plates began to look more like they did in my mind's eye. I rearranged them daily until my quilt approximated my internal vision.

All the plates were hand appliquéd on the background, with a few overlapping the edges. Oops – then I needed a border! I almost quit again, but had put too much work in so far to relegate it to the closet. I looked at my ochre and sienna collections and settled on the Broken Dishes block for a little subtlety.

I machine quilted ROYAL POINCIANAS in time for Hurricane Wilma to devastate our island and our poinciana trees. The quilt and our home survived Wilma. The trees will be back too because they are showing a little green already. Our islands will recover and my quilt will always remind me of the discouragement I overcame while working on it.

A Customized Finish

Once the top was complete, I tried multiple border variations on the computer, but it was difficult to reproduce the center of the quilt to audition the borders. The Broken Dishes block gave movement from curves of the tree and flowers to the angles of the border.

Extra ground and sky were added to make the center fit with the border. Ricky Tims' technique of Quilting Caveman Style was used in the border to overlap the edges of the pieces, cut a gentle curve, and sew the resulting pieces back together.

My mock-up from the computer was used mainly to see how the border worked with the center. I am still learning about the software, but it is much easier than actually making borders to audition. This produces a lot of extra blocks that do eventually find homes, but it is very time consuming and the deadline loomed.

Computer mock-up of ROYAL POINCIANAS

The quilt was finished on my mother's machine because I was taking care of her for a week after surgery and had only two weeks left to complete everything. I even found some great variegated thread to use along with what I had with me. The rainbow thread changes color every 4" and gives a beautiful sheen to the quilting.

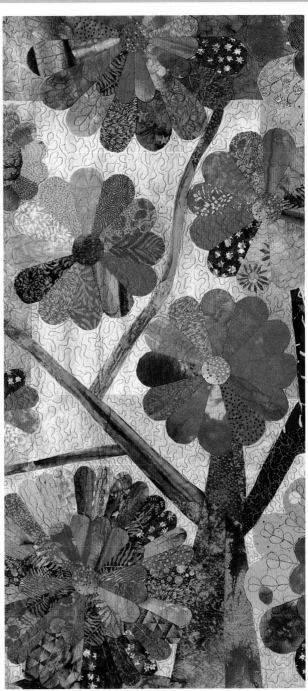

Rainbow thread was used in the quilting to give a beautiful sheen to the quilt.

Ann Feitelson

Montague, Massachusetts

I see myself as both a traditional and contemporary quiltmaker. I enjoy the security of working within a structure or grid. But I also can't resist the temptation to violate it, disrupt it, and play around with it; to bend or break the rules I make. Ultimately, what I'm trying to do is build dramatic abstract compositions that interact with a grid or substructure. The drama comes from color interaction. Color creates dynamic forces. It doesn't just sit there – it has power!

I like to speculate about the origins of different patterns, who the makers of old quilts were, and what ideas they had about the meaning of their work. My guild has a biennial challenge akin to the *New Quilts from an Old Favorite* contest. It chooses a quilt from a local history museum's collection and asks us to use it as the jumping-off point for a new quilt. I enjoy entering that contest just as much as I enjoy entering this one. The present is more meaningful when engaging the past.

Inspiration and Design

I have a 1930s' Dresden Plate quilt that has a brilliant yellow background and an abundance of period fabrics. The scalloped edges of the plates are appliquéd with black blanket-stitching (fig. 1). A MIDSUMMER DAY'S DREAM is a riff on that quilt.

It was summer when I began working on this quilt, and my son was in a production of *A Midsummer Night's Dream.* In that play, anything can happen; craziness rules. As soon as I selected a variety of

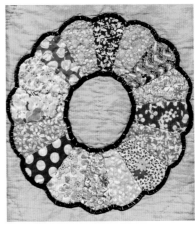

Fig. 1. *One of the 42 blocks from my '30s' inspiration quilt*

Ann's photo by Leah Gans

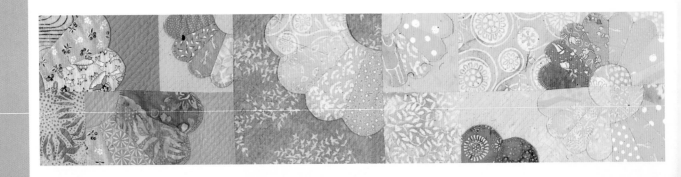

A MIDSUMMER DAY'S DREAM
52½" x 52½"

"Intrigued by the bold effect of the polka-dot fabrics in my 1930s' quilt,
I used as many as I could find. Their effect is dazzling, like after-images of the sun."

yellow fabrics, the quilt seemed to become about the sun – its intoxicating intensity, its primacy in our deepest yearnings.

From the start, I wanted to depart from the traditional by using more than one size of the Dresden Plate block, partial as well as full circles, and an asymmetrical arrangement of small blocks and large blocks. Those elements would provide sufficient shifting complexity to make an interesting composition.

I had never really liked '30s' reproduction fabrics, finding them overly cute, even somewhat repellent. However, when combined with batiks, which I adore, the two very different fabrics complement each other. Both are intense pastels, with motifs of similar sweet nothings. The dissonance of using fabrics that I like and dislike fascinates me.

Nursery rhymes and the whimsical, absurd nature of the reproduction '30s' fabrics accorded with the idea of sun-struck daydreaming, or napping in the sun, which my husband occasionally did on the couch near me in my sewing room. As I worked, I tried to make the quilt more and more radiant. The yellow and yellow-orange areas expanded. The blues and magentas became counter forces representing sky and shadows.

I violated the basic figure-ground relationship of my '30s' quilt by using prints in the background as well as in the plates. Figure-ground consistency is a rule that I like to break. I also do it by obscuring shapes against their backgrounds with similar colors: you'll notice yellow fans on yellow blocks. I get a kick out of that kind of ambiguity.

Finished Curved Edges by Machine

The quilt is entirely machine sewn. Transposing from garment sewing, where facings finish a curved edge, I developed a method of facing the quarter-circles with lightweight interfacing.

After seaming four plate segments, I marked the arched sewing lines with a pencil by tracing around a template, and then machine sewed along the penciled lines with tiny stitches (fig. 2). The area beyond the stitching was clipped and notched with very sharp scissors (fig. 3). Then, the lining was turned to the wrong side and…*voilà*!…a finished curved edge, with no hand sewing (fig. 4).

Fig. 2. *The arched sewing lines were traced from a template, then sewn with tiny stitches.*

Fig. 3. *Sharp scissors were used to clip and notch the area beyond the stitching.*

Figure photos by Leah Gans

Fig. 4. *A finished curved edge was created with no hand sewing.*

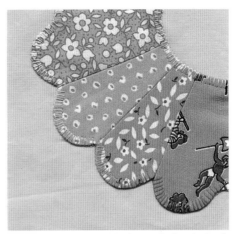

Fig. 5a. *The quarter circle was blanket stitched to the background.*

I wanted to copy the blanket stitching of my original quilt, and was delighted that my machine makes a good facsimile. I put the faced quarter circle on the background block, with tear-away stabilizer behind both, and blanket stitched to attach the quarter circle to the background. The right stroke of the needle went down on the background, the left stroke on the fan. Once the blanket stitching was done, the stabilizer was torn away. I trimmed away both the background block behind the fan and the excess interfacing (fig. 5).

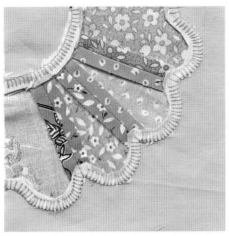

Fig. 5b. *The fabric behind the fan and excess interfacing were trimmed away.*

Finalist

Barbara Oliver Hartman

Flower Mound, Texas

I have always been interested in quilts and do not remember a time when I was not aware of their existence. My grandmother made quilts out of necessity from discarded clothing, and also made them to commemorate special events like graduations, weddings, and babies. My mother was an accomplished seamstress who made beautiful clothing and was well known in our community for her talent.

Mom owned a small dressmaking company, and much of our home life centered on sewing clothing. A couple of times, I dabbled at making a quilt by cutting squares and sewing them together, but my real interest began about 25 years ago. I was looking for a new hobby and had done some knitting, *papier-mâché*, and various other crafts. When I bought my first pattern and fabric for a quilt, the obsession began.

I've been asked, "How do you fit quilting into your busy life?" A better question might be how do I fit other parts of my life into my quilting. Of course,

my first responsibility is my family and taking care of my home. With the kids raised and just my husband and me at home, the responsibilities are not very demanding these days. We love seeing the grandkids and are lucky that most of them live nearby.

Most of my activities are quilt related. I try to spend most days in my studio sewing. Many of my friends are also quiltmakers and I am active in my local guild in Dallas. I go to as many quilt shows a year as possible and rarely miss Paducah or Houston. I cannot see my interest in quiltmaking ending anytime soon.

Inspiration and Design

For the past couple of years, I had been aware of the theme for this year's contest and had dismissed it as something that was too far removed from my usual work. In the spring, I was thinking of making a kaleidoscope-style quilt. My husband and I were on vacation in Santa Fe, and while doodling around with some possible motifs in my sketchbook, a giant Dresden Plate began to appear.

Barbara's photo by Robert Hartman

TWENTY-THREE PLATES
76" x 76"

"Hardly a day goes by that I don't realize what a lucky person I am to get to do what I love and have my friends and family. Life is good!"

By the time we were home, the basic idea was established, and I looked in some books and discovered that Dresden Plates were mostly 16- and 21-wedge designs. I have been making 16-wedge designs for years, so that was my choice. The research also told me that the outer edges of the design could be rounded, scalloped, or pointed.

Using a wedge as my guide, my original idea was to make the outer edge an extra large Dresden Plate, and then make a complicated kaleidoscope for the whole interior design. Soon, the different plates began to appear and it was like a game to see how many Dresden Plate layers could be accomplished while keeping the design innovative and fresh (fig. 1).

Fig. 1. Draft of the Dresden Plate layers

Once the design was set, I drew the full-size shape of the wedge on a piece of muslin and that became my foundation. The design elements were constructed using freezer-paper appliqué. These were also made in layers, and in some places, were as many as four deep before the freezer paper was removed and the muslin cut away.

I chose a background fabric that was bought during quilt show week in Paducah. A random, directional fabric is generally used for the backgrounds on my quilts with circular motifs. They seem to make the central design radiate outward. Fabrics were pulled from my stash to complete the choices. While I like continuity, I also like to use many different fabrics with different textures and shades to add interest.

One practice that I strive to uphold is not to go shopping for a certain fabric once the quilt is started. If I don't have what is needed, substitutions are made with fabrics on hand. This is a practice that has served me well by saving time shopping for the impossible to find. The different fabrics also add interest. I tend to buy batiks and hand-dyed fabrics from other artists, and like to dye and paint some of my own fabrics.

Working out the Wedges

My design sketch started on a 6" square of paper. First, the square was folded diagonally, then in quarters (fig. 2). With a protractor, I made sure that each wedge was 22½ degrees. When making a circular-shaped image with wedges, it is usually necessary to draw/design only one or two of the wedges out to full size. Some of the freezer-paper templates were made from my original line drawing of the wedge (fig. 3).

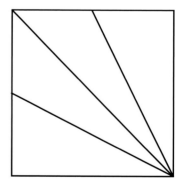

Fig. 2. Square folded in quarters for the design sketch

Fig. 3. *Line drawing from which templates were made*

All of the appliqué was completed with the freezer-paper method and a zigzag stitch with invisible thread. First, a 16-spoke Dresden Plate was made with the pointed shape. Next, a larger 16-spoke Dresden Plate with the rounded shape was made. With the freezer paper still in place, the smaller plate was placed on the larger one and sewn in place. Then, the center was sewn (fig. 4).

Fig. 4. *Assembly sequence*

1. *Starting with the outer edge, the piece was prepared by ironing fabric on freezer paper, and then stitching it in place.*

2. *This piece was prepared and stitched the same as the first.*

3. *This piece, including the circle, was added next.*

4. *These rounded wedges were then added.*

5. *These pointed wedges were added after they were sewn together.*

6. *Adding these plates was the last step before the wedges were connected.*

Finalist

Barbara Holtzman

Holyoke, Colorado

My first quilting project was a hand-pieced bed quilt that took over five years to complete. After coming across a miniature quilting magazine, I knew right away that this was something I could enjoy. A small quilt could be completed more quickly, right? I found out that smaller quilts actually take a lot of time because you need to be more precise.

I make as many small quilts as my time permits, and can actually finish them. The good thing about small quilts is they challenge me to be better at cutting, matching seams, pressing, and all the details that go into a good quilt. I also see where making a small version of a big quilt is a good way to try new ideas without the time and expense of a larger quilt.

I like to search the Internet, and it's a wonderful way to view new quilts. It is great for inspiration and gives me new ideas of inventive ways to use fabric. I especially like some of the art quilts, and enjoy using old patterns in new and interesting ways, which is why this challenge appeals to me. There is always something new and exciting to do with fabric – I have so much left to try! While I enjoy my day job, it has nothing to do with quilting, and I find quilting and designing a good creative outlet.

Inspiration and Design

I've admired many old quilts that use the Dresden Plate. Quilting time is a precious commodity with a full-time job, a husband, and kids. I was able to hand sew many of the flowers during my morning and afternoon breaks at work. It's amazing what can be done in 15 minutes if you're prepared. Goals and deadlines were constantly being set with this quilt. It was a challenging and rewarding process. It became almost obsessive to me – I went to bed dreaming and planning the next part and spent spare time sketching and wondering what would happen if I did something different.

After deciding on a design, the quilt took almost a year to make. It changed direction several times. I tried to think of new ways to use the Dresden Plate and because it looks like a flower, that's the direction I took. The kaleidoscope-style seemed like a natural choice, using the petals for repeats.

The hardest part was finding the right material for the petals. I made a clear plastic template to view and cut fabric for the Dresden Plate, and wanted to use material that you wouldn't ordinarily associate with flowers. I came across a couple of fish prints and a Hawaiian print that seemed suitable. Once a few were fussy cut, I knew I was on the right track. It was fun to imagine how the flower would look by

Barbara's photo by Ellie Lock

MY PSYCHEDELIC GARDEN

62" x 62"

*"Quilters have said how their quilts tell them what to do, and I wasn't sure
I believed them until making this quilt. All along it seemed to almost create itself."*

one little petal, but it was even more fun to hand piece the flower and see the end result. They were wild – psychedelic even.

The original design was to have a fence around the flower garden, but that seemed too confining for these flowers. The fence would have required less

Dresden Plates were fussy cut from fish and Hawaiian prints.

time, but I was at the point of no return. I changed to a scalloped border of grass, with bits of the flowers showing through; it was more time-consuming, but definitely more fitting with the idea.

This was an enjoyable and challenging quilt. I would like to try to make another quilt using just 4" flowers, but with a more quiet fabric. I think a fence might work with quieter flowers – but I'll let the quilt decide.

Pairing Flowers with Backgrounds

Basting around the outside of each pieced flower ensured nice round petals. Then, the flowers were pressed with a hot iron and starch, while I opened the seams and carefully pressed the roundness of the petals. The starch really helped to flatten them out.

I had picked a grassy type material for the background, but the green was just too boring. Different greens were needed, so I created a paper-pieced pattern of grass blades radiating from the flowers. Just thinking of pulling out all those little strips of paper made me queasy. Then, I saw Judy Mathieson on *Simply Quilts*, and she showed her pattern for radiating stars using freezer paper. So I decided to needle my pattern on freezer paper, and pieced with 12–15 different green material strips. It worked great, and the best part – no paper to pull out!

The green background material was starched, cut into 1¼" strips, and carefully paper pieced by sewing right next to the fold of the freezer paper. The strips were cut to length as they were sewn. The strips should be about ¼" longer at the middle of the pattern and about ½" longer on the outside of the pattern, to allow for seam allowance later.

Once each background strip had been sewn and the circle joined, I basted just outside the square before removing the freezer paper. After removing the freezer paper, I starched and pressed again. The freezer-paper pattern can be used several times.

When the grass block was complete, the flower was carefully centered and hand sewn. From behind, the grass was trimmed about ⅜" from the flower edge. The flower and grass block were centered on a piece of batting larger than the flower. I basted just outside the petal around the flower from the front using wash-away thread. On the back again, the batting was trimmed close to the wash-away stitching and the block was cut to size. Once the quilt top was completely done and sandwiched, I used invisible thread to sew again on top of the wash-away thread, locking down the extra batting.

The same process was used for the scallops and the border corners, only this time, I used one strip of the fish prints in almost every scallop to add color and excitement.

Needle-punch freezer paper pattern

An occasional strip of the fish print adds a splash of color to the scalloped border.

Finalist

Ann Horton

Redwood Valley, California

You could say my quilting career spans my life-time. I can remember helping Grandma with the quilting needles as a young girl, and then some 20 years ago, I became passionate about quilting and have not paused since. A heartland farm girl trans-planted to the west coast, I live in a rural mountain setting in northern California and am ever inspired by nature.

My husband grows wonderful gardens, and this feast of the senses weaves its flavor into my work. We have emphasized hands-on creativity in our lives, and I feel that quilting is an important way to connect with my heart and hands. I am grateful for God's gift of creativity in my life, and purposefully provide myself with ample time and space to honor the importance of my artistic endeavors.

One year ago, I took over two rooms of our house and created my dream studio. One room was devoted to shelving that holds my fabric collection. Working with my fabric in view has been a great aid in pulling colors and adding the unexpected piece that moves the quilt forward. The second room holds my sewing space. I purposefully made this room a rich mixture of color and shape, and it is my favorite place to sit and dream in free-flowing creativity.

The windows of my studio overlook an expanse of sweeping valley and mountain horizons. This space has signified for me the vast importance for an artist to believe in oneself and to take one's work seriously. This life offers the abundant choice of priority as to how we spend our time and talent. I find that quilting soothes and excites, frustrates and in turn, provides a rich sense of satisfaction when the work is done. It is a blessing to not only create, but to be able to share the creation with the world.

Inspiration and Design

TRIBAL FEAST began with a chimpanzee. After finishing another quilt with thread-painted fox, I decided to continue my thread-painting technique on a whole animal in action. This little guy started as a piece of brown fabric with a soft brown face, and soon I had a full, smiling, and friendly imp in my sewing room. I loved this chimp's personality and was happy to have him hang out on my design wall. I knew he would have a quilt to call home at some point, but was not sure what direction that would take.

I had a large stash of African fabrics, and felt those textiles would be a good match for my monkey. In thinking about the upcoming Dresden Plate contest, it came to me that the fabrics would be great fun to pair into an assortment of African plates.

Ann's photo by Jessica Horton

TRIBAL FEAST

75" x 75"

"Hiking in God's glorious creation allows me to absorb the textures, colors, and expanse of this life, and I try to include this complexity in my art."

The center design of the quilt was created by printing out several variations of the Dresden Plate block from my BlockBase program. Because I have a hard time following rules, I immediately created my own variations. I love to embellish with machine embroidery, so the blocks had large centers that could hold designs. Designs were selected that seemed tribal to me, reflecting the bold and sometimes primitive feel of African textiles, pottery, and weavings.

I wanted a border that would give the chimp a natural setting, such as a jungle with foliage and more embroidery. I drew a spiked border with curved corners that would give me more space to play with the landscape of my jungle. After completing this border, I knew it had to be set off of the center with a bit of turquoise, so the small homespun border was added. This gave me a place to do some beading and quilting. I loved what was happening with the rich colors and textures.

Another thread painting was needed to help balance the chimp in the top corner. The blue-sky background was changed into water and the hippo was born. The bottom "water" corners balanced the turquoise, and gave enough space for more embroidery. The final Guatemalan fabric border was my palette for border embroidery.

Although the quilt was pretty much done at this point, it just wouldn't let me be. More primitive stitching and African beads and shells kept calling me, so I began the time-consuming task of hand couching silk sari yarns around each of the plates, as well as weaving them into the upper vines of the jungle. Lush wool yarns were hand stitched around each of the plate centers to add more texture. Smaller variegated yarns were hand quilted into the turquoise border, and then beading and African cowrie shells were added to the plates.

Embroideries of African masks and salamanders were added to the borders, along with African painted beads. The final step was to name the quilt, and

TRIBAL FEAST seemed perfect. Not only did it play off the plate theme, but also this quilt really was a feast of techniques, colors, and textures.

Thread Painting Basics

Thread painted chimp

Thread painting is a technique that requires patience, a lot of practice, and even more thread. The chimp's realistic fur was achieved with layers upon layers of various-colored threads. The batik used for his face, ear, hands, and feet was shaped and stitched to create features and dimension. I added light stuffing to his face because this feature had popped forward while thread painting, creating tension around the face. I like this aspect of the chimp.

The realistic body pose of hanging from the vine gives the chimp lifelike grace and personality. Twisting and hand couching the silk sari threads together to create the vines kept the threads' texture and loft sufficient to complement the chimp's dimensional presence. When painting the animals, I worked on a separate piece of layered batting and fabric (fig. 1). The piece was then trimmed and "painted" with thread into the quilt setting (fig. 2).

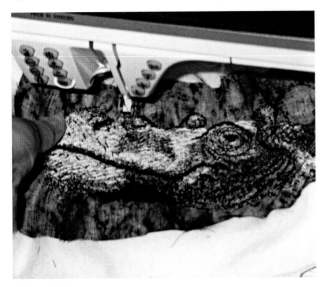

Fig. 1. The animals were created on a separate piece of fabric.

Fig. 2. The completed thread painting was then "painted" into the quilt setting.

Pairing digitized embroidery motifs with the free-hand thread painting is a fun way to play with your machine's capabilities and to add great details that enrich the quilt's surface. The berries, flowers, and butterflies were added to the quilt to overlap leaves and background, making them realistic to the viewer (fig. 3). I am careful to select designs that feel authentic to the quilt. All designs in TRIBAL FEAST are from the Husqvarna/Viking embroidery collection.

Fig. 3. Berries, flowers, and butterflies overlap elements in the background.

While most people would think of fabric choices as the main color statement in a quilt, the thread colors chosen for embroidery are like the painting flourishes that highlight and enrich the surface in unexpected ways. A delicate dance of embellishment, color, and texture is a balance that either makes the quilt or detracts. It helps to establish a theme or feel that carries through the whole making of the quilt. In TRIBAL FEAST, the repetition of the plate blocks and the constant variations of the colors and embellishments make for a drumbeat of movement and rhythm throughout the quilt.

Finalist

Agnete Kay

Calgary, Alberta, Canada

Embroidery was my passion for many years. At age 16, I designed my own cross-stitch patterns. Then, in the late 1980s, I had the opportunity for a closer look at quiltmaking while taking some classes, subscribing to quilting magazines, and attending quilt shows. It soon became clear that quilting was my new passion.

Quiltmaking seems to offer more variety of visual effects than embroidery. I am not in any way favorable of the idea that faster is better, but one has to admit that it is, in most cases, quicker to make a quilt of nine square feet than to embroider a piece of similar size. So by designing and making quilts, I could depict in colorful cloth more of my life experiences, shall we say, than by embroidering.

The time of life is upon me when age slows one down much more than expected. Thus, I am not as prolific as I was, but still have half a dozen projects going at all times, and even finish some from time to time. Whether sewing or not, I have such a great time being a grandmother, not to mention being a mother and mother-in-law, that each new day is a lovely gift.

Inspiration and Design

As soon as I looked closely at the classic Dresden Plate block, it reminded me of a daisy. The daisy is known in many European and Latin American languages as the *marguerite*. I decided that my approach with this quilt would be to make something with daisies. The idea of making it a reminder of childhood pastimes, namely making a Daisy Chain, began to develop.

For a long time, I had a vague plan of doing something with all my many red cotton scraps, perhaps with the addition of other colors in the spectrum close to red, such as violet and orange. Red would be a perfect background for the white and yellow daisies, so red scraps it was.

I had once tried the Dresden Plate pattern, and the wedges had a tendency to lean sideways so that the seams did not point to the central circle. To avoid this pitfall, I developed an effective method of construction. Others may have done it this way forever, but it was new to me and has worked well. Since making this Daisy Chain, I have made one other daisy quilt, VIVE LA MARGUERITE II (page 58).

Once upon a time, Gerald Roy said that one reason quilting is so popular is because with a square design, such as a block, you just cannot go wrong. It always looks good. Other geometric shapes can be much harder to make appealing. After starting with a square followed by a border of hearts, I decided to add further borders to the top and bottom only, making the whole quilt rectangular, just to make it a little easier to go wrong! It worked out quite well, and the curved silk strip and the edge echo the Daisy Chain.

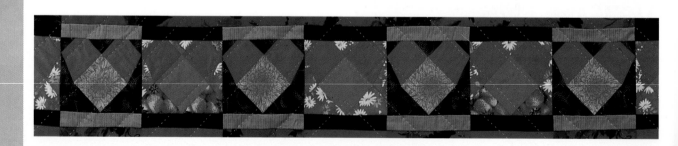

VIVE LA MARGUERITE – DAISY CHAIN
63" x 74"

"The rose is romantic, the lily is mysterious, but the daisy is a cheerful flower. It is also the flower of Denmark, the country where I was born, and it remains one of my favorite flowers."

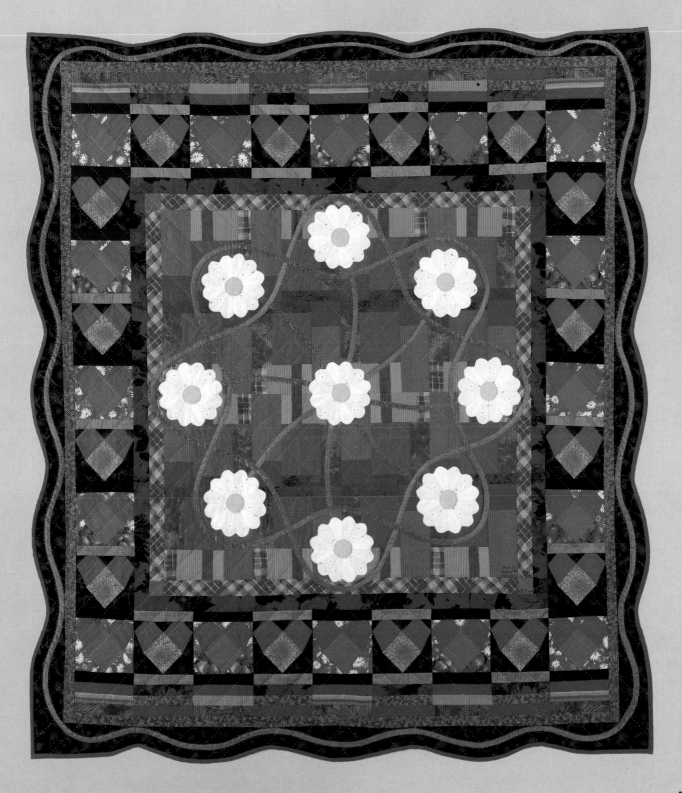

VIVE LA MARGUERITE II

Creating the Daisy Chain

First, I drafted a simple block of squares and triangles, Mondrian-like, so to speak. From that pattern, I sewed 16 blocks and put them together so that each row of four blocks was in the opposite direction of the previous row. There was just enough of my favorite orange ikat plaid to make a 2" border around the 16-block square.

Then it was time for the daisies. For a total of 12 wedges or petals per circle, each petal needs to be 30 degrees. Using a protractor, a cardboard template was drawn. I drew along a coin to make the wide end of the wedge rounded. With a sharp pencil, I traced four petals per daisy on the back of three different white prints. The petals were cut out with a seam allowance on all sides, including the curve. This would help prevent too much fraying during the handling and sewing of the petals.

The petals were pinned and stitched along the pencil line by machine from the rounded edge to the very point of the narrow end. It was best to stitch three together first, then six, and then the full 12. The center where the seams met were bulky, but sewing right to the tip helped all the petals point straight toward the middle. Once all the petals were joined, the bulky part in the middle was snipped off, leaving a ½" hole.

After pressing all seams open, the seam allowances were trimmed off the rounded edges to the pencil line. Each daisy was placed on a slightly larger piece of prewashed flannelette. It was smoothed in all directions until flat, and then pinned down. The flannelette added body and prevented the dark background fabric from being visible.

The yellow flower center was traced with a pencil, and then cut out on the pencil line. With matching yellow thread, I stitched the circle on the daisy with a satin stitch. Carefully moving the flower, stitches securely and completely covered the edge, not leaving any fraying visible. To prevent unsightly pulling of the fabrics, I placed a sheet of white paper under the fabric when satin stitching. The paper ripped off easily afterward.

To link the daisies into a chain, I cut about 25 yards of 1" wide bias tape. A yard of violet silk that contrasted with the red was used. The strip was pressed in half with the wrong side inward so both right sides were folded in and met in the middle (fig. 1). With the open-edged side down, eight strips or stalks of equal length were cut and pinned to the quilt top with a slight curve for an organic effect. They were sewn in place with regular stitches close to both edges of the strip.

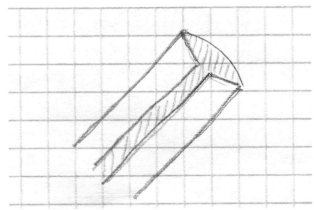

Fig. 1. To press the bias strip, two edges were folded in and held with one hand, while the iron was moved slowly across the strip.

With sharp scissors, the flannelette was trimmed behind the daisies so it followed the outline of the petals. The daisies were pinned in place on the red background, one covering the end of the stalks in the middle, the others placed the same distance from the middle, each covering the other end of a stalk. With a satin stitch and white thread, the daisies were stabilized with paper underlay and sewn to the background.

For the chain effect, bias binding was sewn around the daisies the same way as the stalks. Where two ends met, they were joined as neatly and securely as possible.

A border of 32 heart blocks in two different colorways was pieced. This was followed by a border design of narrow rectangles on the top and bottom and just one narrow strip on the sides. Then, a wider purple border was added on all sides, on which the remaining bias strips were sewn in a curved effect

(fig. 2). This strip was pinned on the quilt top three different ways before I was satisfied.

Fig. 2. *Remaining bias strips from the Dresden Plates were added to the purple border.*

The quilt was then layered with cotton batting and backing, and hand quilted in a long stitch. The purple border was cut in a curved line following the violet bias strip, but the corners were left square. Bias-cut binding finished the quilt.

Chris Lynn Kirsch

Watertown, Wisconsin

It is hard to believe what a huge part of my life quilting has become. My mother taught me to sew as a child and I enjoyed sewing for my family for many years. It wasn't until 1987 that I even considered quilting. We had recently moved to a new area and my sister-in-law invited me to take a class. She never finished her first quilt, but I became an addict.

I jumped in with a passion, but was limited to following patterns without a background in art. With the encouragement of some great teachers, I discovered an unexpected artistic side of myself.

Along with this new direction, I began to teach classes and eventually made the leap from dental hygienist to quilt teacher. Teaching led to lecturing and presenting programs, which in turn led to quilting cruises. My most recent adventure was taking a group of quilters on a riverboat cruise along the Danube in Europe.

I couldn't pursue my passion without the support and encouragement of my wonderful husband. I feel the greatest inspiration in my work is my loving family, my faith in Christ, and the beauty of God's world. My hope is that my quilts will touch others, and my classes will encourage quilters to discover their own style and the artist within.

Contests and challenges are a great way to kick-start a new project. The wonderful part about being a quilting teacher is that I don't have to fit quilting into my life, and now that my children are grown, it is much easier to pursue quilting full time. When quilting, I can say, "I'm working." What a wonderful job!

Inspiration and Design

I have been intrigued by the *New Quilts from an Old Favorite* contest since its inception and have been inspired to enter numerous times. My first reaction to this year's Dresden Plate pattern was less than enthusiastic. Some of the previous year's blocks tickled my imagination as soon as I read about them, but not this time. I didn't feel the urge to stretch or skew the block, and the pattern seemed to scream "muslin and calico."

Then it hit me: don't change the block, simply use contemporary fabric and see what happens. I challenged myself to use only one black and one multicolor batik fabric. Strategic cutting left me with three yards of batik that resembled Swiss cheese – wonder what I'll do with this new challenge.

In the past, I have made traditional Dresden Plate quilts using piecing and appliqué, but felt this contemporary version should employ contemporary techniques. Thus, the blocks were made simply by

DRESDEN PLATE GLASS WINDOW
50" x 69"

"By strategically cutting the blades from multicolor fabric and quilting with high-contrast thread, the result was a stained-glass window look that seems to have a multitude of fabrics instead of just two."

fusing the blades onto a large black background square, leaving a space for the black fabric to show through between them.

Quilting in neon thread around the plates

Couching over plates in black thread

The most challenging part of this quilt was couching thick black perle cotton thread over the blades. I chose to use a narrow zigzag stitch with fine black thread and no feed dogs. The entire process would have been considerably easier if I had three arms. The free-motion machine couching was a tenuous activity I wouldn't recommend for the weak at heart.

By quilting one block at a time, the quilting was stress free and an entirely enjoyable experience. I marked the edges of each area to be quilted with a sliver of soap. This is my favorite marking tool because it is inexpensive, shows well on black, and removes easily. The marked lines were stitched in black thread and the open areas were quilted with neon threads. I love to free-motion quilt, but this was not always the case. It took me years of practice to find the fun in it. When there is joy in the process, it shows.

I was extremely pleased with the stained-glass window quilt that resulted from a less than enthusiastic beginning and a lot of untried techniques and

ideas. I'm very happy with this quilt, and having it accepted in this contest was the icing on the cake.

Creating Couching Designs

I wanted to come up with a different design for each plate. This sounded simple until I stared at the blocks and nothing came to mind. To work through this creative block, designs were tested on the Dresden Plates with a piece of acetate overlay film and a black washable marker. I could create, erase, and recreate the designs in the blades and see how the design would look on top of the fabric colors and patterns through the acetate.

The couching designs were created as follows (refer to the illustration on page 63):

1. This was one of the few designs I did freehand. After years of practicing free-motion quilting, more designs are within my range of abilities. I doodled quite a few designs before deciding on this one.

2. Designs that connected visually with the next blade when identical blades were set side by side were very pleasing. After drawing a heart at the top of one blade, I experimented with side-to-side lines that met with adjacent blades. The slight curves in this version appealed to me.

3. This design was ad-libbed with just a ruler and a few freehand curves to connect the lines.

4. Two different-size leaf templates were used for this design. By drawing around templates, these designs were simple to transfer to the fabric.

5. These arcs were made by tracing different-size circles.

6. Portions of bigger circle templates were drawn to achieve large arcs in the blades. Once again, these lines connected well with adjacent blades when identical blades were set side by side.

When creating couching designs, you can go through kitchen and desk drawers to find different-size circles or other shapes to trace around. An easier option is to use June Tailor's Mix'n Match Templates for Quilters™, which contains different sizes of one simple shape.

To transfer the non-template designs to the block, I created my own template by tracing the shape onto the dull side of freezer paper, cutting it out, and ironing it in place on the quilt block. For the first design, I skipped drawing directly on the fabric and couched along the edge of the paper pattern. I was then able to peel the pattern off and iron it in place on the next blade.

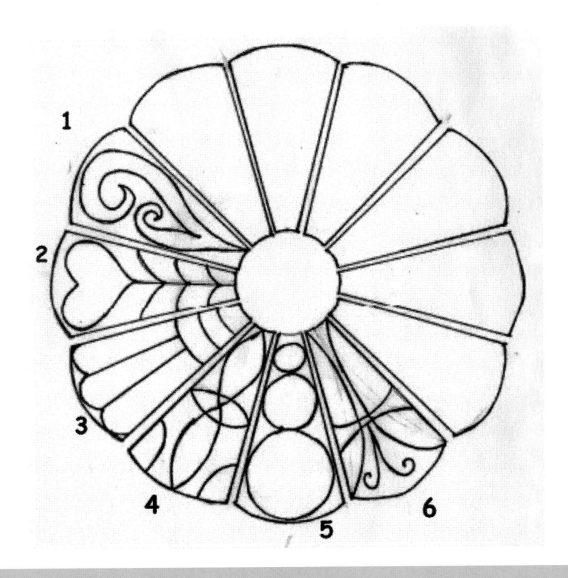

Finalist

Carolee Miller
Centennial, Colorado

Many changes have been brought to my life since my youngest daughter left the nest last year for college. Although my husband and I miss our three girls being home, I do appreciate the extra time for quilting, commission work, and teaching quilt classes.

To sum up my passion, I love quilting, almost to the exclusion of everything else. As most quilters would agree, I find inspiration just about everywhere – Colorado, family, events, nature, art, and other quilters. I quilt as often as possible, but sometimes life gets in the way. My machine is always ready to use, even if there are only a few minutes available.

I have found that while working on one project, I get ideas for many more quilts. Sometimes they make it past the idea state and into a finished product, but there are always ideas swirling around in my head. Periodically, I like to push myself beyond my capabilities, and am often pleased with the results.

From a professional standpoint, I have been doing commission work in addition to being a home seamstress for *Quiltmaker* magazine for 15 years. As a quilting teacher, my highlight in this arena has been teaching weekend retreats in the Rocky Mountains through quilt shops in the Denver area. I am also proud of the fact that all three of my daughters know how to quilt.

Inspiration and Design

I have followed this contest for years and am always amazed by the creativity and quality of the winning quilts. Piecing being my first love, the Dresden Plate contest was somewhat out of my comfort zone. After spending some time thinking about it, I wondered if the pattern could be oval shaped. The quilt evolved rapidly from this initial vision.

It was a challenge to draft the wedge patterns, but exciting to freehand cut the outer edges, the center diamond, and the lighter green background. I had wanted to include a number of miniature plates, but had difficulty making it work until realizing that they could be quilted as a smaller version of the large plate in the dark green border triangles.

The large Dresden Plate was drafted with 16 wedges rather than the traditional 12 due to its large scale. The wedges were made up of batiks from my stash, plus fabrics from a couple trips to the quilt shop. Some of my purchases were more successful than others, but all was not lost because those extra pieces now make up the quilt back.

The quilt went into "time out" a number of times while I struggled with the next step. The quilt took on the look of a flying carpet early on, so I knew it would need fringe on the top and bottom edges. I liked the thought of beads for the fringe,

Carolee's photo by Aie Mindieta, Glamour Shots

DRESDEN FLYING CARPET

56½" x 67½"

"I have always loved quilts, along with the act of creating something that allows freedom of expression and is tangible enough to pass on to my loved ones."

but had no experience or clue how to make it a reality. In addition to the bead embellishment, decorative yarn was couched around the light-green background for emphasis.

Hand beading was perhaps the greatest challenge of this quilt because I rarely do handwork and usually even consider sewing down a hanging sleeve a hardship. There was trial and error in figuring out how to bead, then convincing my fingers to limber up and cooperate during the process. Amazingly, the greatest challenge turned out to be my favorite part. I am proud of the finished product and honored to be a finalist in this competition.

Beading Embellishment and Fringe

Beading on the flower centers of the large Dresden Plate was done with hand quilting thread, a needle small enough to go through the beads, and small seed beads. I placed three to five orange beads and one yellow bead on the thread, then positioned the beads as desired. The needle was inserted in the fabric at the end of the beads, then moved between the quilt layers, coming up near the center of the flower to start the next line of beads (fig. 1).

After the last line of beads, the needle was pulled through to the back. With a tiny backstitch, I pulled the needle through the loop and thread to create a knot. The needle was then inserted through the layers in the same spot, coming up about ½" beyond the knot. I gave the thread a tug, listening for a little pop, to bury the knot in the layers.

For the fringe, a variety of small glass beads were used. A combination of black and purple, some of these beads were rounded and some faceted and varied in length. I wanted the beads on the fringe to be random, so they were all poured into a bowl and mixed. I began by burying the knot in the binding, then running the needle through the beads several times, picking up assorted beads with each pass until the desired fringe length was achieved.

The thread was wrapped around the last bead, then the needle was put back through the other beads and back into the binding at the starting point, coming up about ¼" away to begin the next fringe (fig. 2, page 67). The thread was pulled snug so the fringe would stand out from the binding edge (fig. 3, page 67). Near the end of the row, adjust spacing so that the fringes are spaced appropriately. Some of the individual fringes are a bit longer than others, but this gave the quilt more of that carpet look I was seeking.

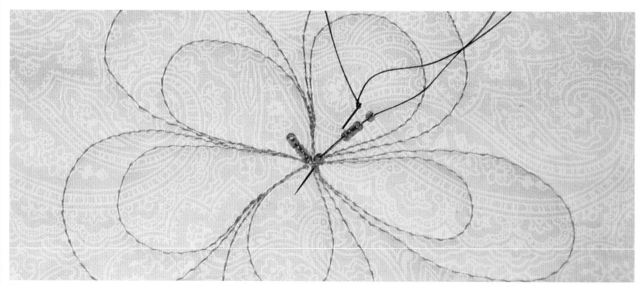

Fig. 1. Threaded with beads, the needle was inserted between the quilt layers, coming up near the flower center.

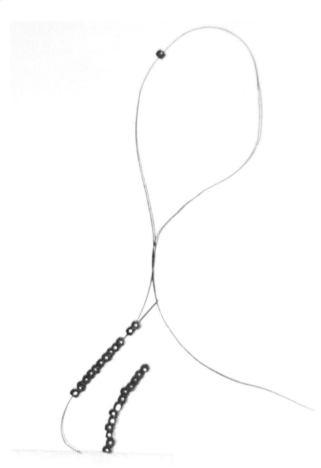

Fig. 2. *To secure the fringe, the thread was wrapped around the last bead and put back through the other beads. Then the needle was inserted in the binding once again.*

Fig. 3. *The thread was pulled snug so the fringe would stand out.*

Hand beading adds to the ornate charm of DRESDEN FLYING CARPET.

Claudia Clark Myers
& Jessica Torvinen

Duluth, Minnesota

Claudia Clark Myers

Jessica Torvinen

My mother was a costume designer for ballet and opera, and was always at her sewing machine. She taught me to sew when I was very young, but quilting was foreign to me until I was pregnant with my second son. My mom was working on a quilt for him, and I thought it looked interesting.

I asked her to show me how to piece a block and that was it. I took the rest of the pieces home and finished the top. I was hooked! I am married with three sons and have a busy life, so my sewing is usually done at night after everyone is in bed. That first quilt was 13 years ago, and since then, I have made many quilts, entered several contests, and even won a few ribbons.

I worked at a local quilt shop awhile ago when the owner purchased a longarm quilting machine. I always wanted to work from home like my mom, and machine quilting seemed like the perfect solution. In 2004, I bought that longarm from the shop and have been quilting as a business from home ever since.

I really enjoy custom machine quilting and have developed my own style. This is the first important piece my mom has asked me to quilt and I was honored to do it with her. She is creative and talented, and just being with her is inspiring. I would like to be able to spend more time quilting, but for now, I'm just learning from the wonderful quilters around me.

Claudia Clark Myers

When my daughter Jess was a teenager, the only sewing she really liked to do was to make something fast, to wear out that night. She called them "whip-up clothes" and even then, I could see a lot of ingenuity at work as she figured out how to simplify the patterns.

Both of her brothers could sew too. They put together their own Halloween costumes, went through the down shirt kit stage, and now the oldest, Tad, can make alterations on a kilt – no problem! His brother, Pete, was the mainstay pillow maker back when I had an at-home cottage industry. Because I was always at the machine, it was natural for them to gravitate to sewing, and it was a pleasure to see that they were using a skill I had taught them.

My great, great grandmother was a quilter. I have a snapshot taken in about 1918 when she was quite old, standing in front of a quilt that hung on a clothesline. The caption reads "Grandmother Clark and one of her quilts she always made," probably written by my grandmother. Both of my grandmothers sewed, one for enjoyment and one for a living. I learned from both of them.

My mother sewed and she taught me. I remember sitting under the kitchen table, where she sewed on her Featherweight, piecing together discarded scraps to make doll clothes. Having taught Jess to sew, I now watch her make her quilts and quilt for other people, and I learn from her. Now, Jess has taught her boys to sew and all three have each made a quilt that was featured in the book *Quilts from the Quiltmaker's Gift.*

Claudia and Jessica's photo by Jeffrey D. Frey

SERVICE FOR TWELVE

78" x 78"

"Even more important than finishing and entering this quilt,
the best thing is that we were fortunate to be able to do it together."

Inspiration and Design

I think about this contest every year. Some years, I have a design in mind that would be great to do. Three times, I have finished the quilt and gotten it in on time and have been included in the book and exhibit. Many more times, other things get in the way, and before I know it, the deadline has come and gone and the quilt is still in my head.

Determined to make the deadline this year, I had thought of a way to simplify the Dresden Plate pattern. I paper piece for many reasons, but mainly, because I am not very accurate at cutting and sewing. Too many years of my life were spent designing and sewing costumes, where 3" seams are the norm. The motto was always "done is good" and if the little mistakes don't show when you are sitting in the third row, then that's enough.

I was sure the concept of paper piecing would apply to the Dresden Plate block by sewing sections of it, and then using what I call control templates to trim and assure accuracy. This block was designed so that the petals of the plate are staggered and don't need to meet at any point. Another trick was to appliqué a motif over the center where all the points come together, trimming away the fabric underneath. This way, the center points don't have to meet perfectly either – sort of akin to sewing a button in the center of a Mariner's Compass.

However, none of this would have mattered if I couldn't meet the deadline, but I had a secret weapon – the other member of my team. I'm proud to say that my daughter has become a very good longarm machine quilter. I knew she was going to finish it on time, and she did, beautifully.

Making a Block with Control Templates

Audition and assemble all your fabrics, and make a swatch board (fig. 1). Make sure you have enough contrast between light and dark fabrics in each plate. Keep the swatches for each plate together and decide how many of each plate you are going to make.

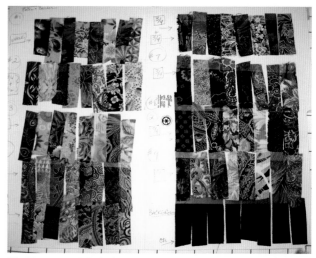

Fig. 1. A swatch board helps to audition and assemble fabrics.

Make all your templates (page 72–73) and transfer any markings. Using figure 2 as a reference, cut a cardboard template from the curved parts of templates A and C and laminate them.

Cut templates A–D from the light and dark fabrics. Cut 2½" x 6" extensions for the shorter wedges from the background fabric. Also cut the frame template from the background fabric.

Using the laminated cardboard templates, mark the curve on the A and C pieces where the petals will sit. Spray starch into a small bowl and use a paintbrush to wet the curved top edge of the petals. Turn ¼" over the cardboard templates and press with a hot iron (fig. 2).

Fig. 2. Use the laminated cardboard templates to mark the curves and turn the curved seams.

Place the petal on top of its dark background piece, matching the top curved edge of the petal to the marked line on the background. Pin in place. Sew around the petal edges with a zigzag stitch. Sew a 6" rectangle to the top of each C piece. Using the wedge control template, mark and trim all edges of each paddle (fig. 3).

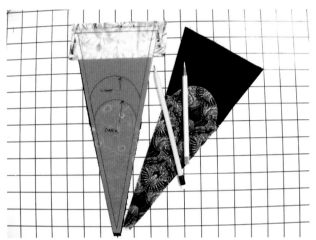

Fig. 3. Mark and trim the edges of each paddle with the wedge control template.

Sew the paddles together in sets of four. Using the blade fan control template, mark and trim the top curved edge of the paddle unit (fig. 4).

Fig. 4. Mark and trim the top curved edge of the paddle unit.

Clip the curved edge of the light background frame very closely, at least every ¼". Clip almost to the ¼" seam line, but not quite.

Pin the center of the frame and the center of the quarter plate section right sides together. Pin each end. Sew a ¼" seam joining the frame and the quarter plate, having the frame side up, pushing the clipped edges out to match the plate edges as you sew. Pull slightly on both layers as you sew, easing the two layers together and keeping the edges perfectly even (fig. 5).

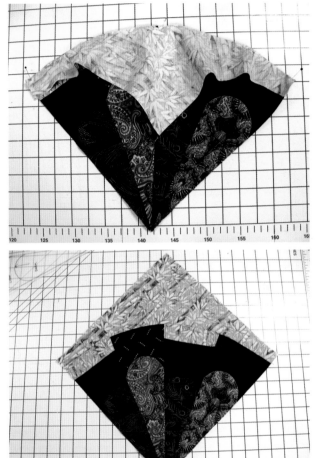

Fig. 5. Sew the frame and quarter plate section together.

Assemble the blocks as shown in the quilt picture, and sew the quilt together in horizontal rows.

Cut out a fabric motif, place it on iron-on fusible web, and draw around it. Cut away the fusible in the center, leaving about ¼" around the outside edge. Fuse the motif to the quilt and sew around the edges with a zigzag stitch.

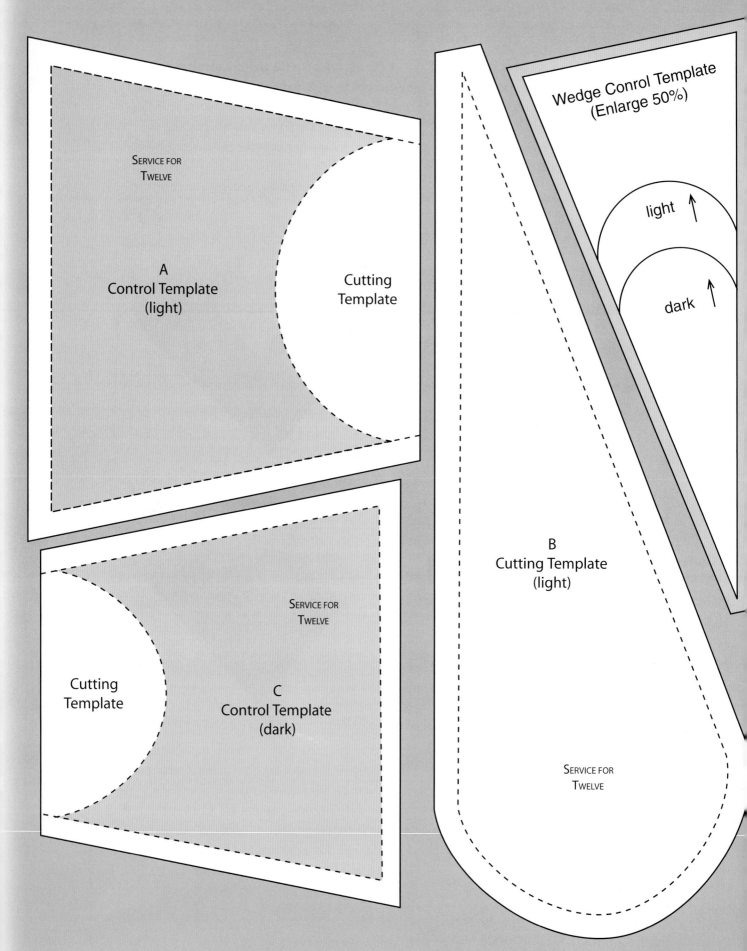

SERVICE FOR
TWELVE

A
Control Template
(light)

Cutting
Template

Wedge Conrol Template
(Enlarge 50%)

light

dark

B
Cutting Template
(light)

Cutting
Template

C
Control Template
(dark)

SERVICE FOR
TWELVE

SERVICE FOR
TWELVE

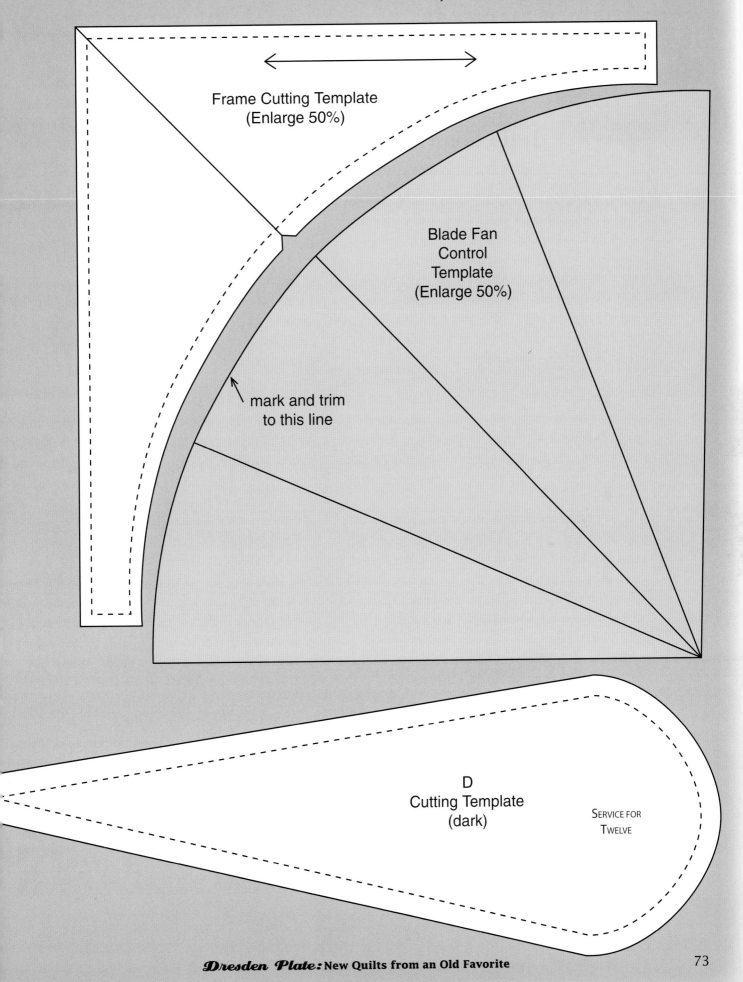

Frame Cutting Template
(Enlarge 50%)

Blade Fan
Control
Template
(Enlarge 50%)

mark and trim
to this line

D
Cutting Template
(dark)

SERVICE FOR
TWELVE

Finalist

Judy Sogn

Seattle, Washington

Quilting means so many things to me. My best friends are quilters. I watch television shows on quilting for new ideas and quilt in the evening while "watching" television with my husband. Quilting projects go with me whenever I travel, and when traveling, quilt shops are used as rest stops along the way. I have about 20 quilts hanging in my house at any one time and change many of them to fit the season or holiday.

I am constantly inspired by the quilts in books, magazines, at quilt guild show and tell, and at quilt shows. I like to take ideas from several sources and combine or alter them to make my own statement, which is one reason that I enjoy this contest. It challenges me to try new techniques, new colors, and new sets.

My best friends are quilters, and every January six of us pack our gear and head to the beach. We rent a beautiful house on Hood Canal. We started over 12 years ago with a three-day retreat. A few years later, we increased it to five days, and then in a few more years, seven days. On our tenth anniversary, someone suggested that we should celebrate with 10 days. That was so much fun that we decided to continue 10 days every year.

We load three vans with sewing machines, laptop computers, printers, irons, oversized ironing tables, embroidery machines, office chairs, sewing tables, sergers, fabric and notions, movies, food, and clothes. We only leave the house for more groceries or for an excursion to a nearby quilt shop.

This is a tradition that all of us look forward to all year long, and one that we will continue forever. We have even discussed hiring grandchildren to help with the heavy lifting. My non-quilting friends are amazed that we spend 10 days sewing and that six women have remained such close friends all these years. Quilters understand.

Inspiration and Design

For several years, I have been inspired by the *New Quilts from an Old Favorite* contest. I like the idea of reinterpreting an old pattern and adding my own style. Another favorite aspect of the contest is seeing all the interpretations of the same design. It is truly amazing to see the wide range of styles that result from the same pattern.

The fabrics for DOTTIE DRESDEN are all polka dots, including the backing, label, and binding. It was a bit of a challenge to find enough variation of dotted fabrics in the colors I wanted, which was a great excuse to fabric shop.

Because I love foundation paper piecing and Dresden Plates are usually appliquéd, I used computer quilt design software to draw a paper-pieced plate. Drawing the design on the computer was easy and it allowed me to piece with straight lines.

DOTTIE DRESDEN

52½" x 52½"

"I was concerned that all the bright colors and busy polka dots would be a confused jumble, but I think the final result is playful and it reminds me of a circus carrousel."

The color pallet was based on the wonderful hot-pink polka dot fabric in the main background. Black and white was used in the center of the plates to add contrast and drama. Once I started piecing, I realized the 16 pieces coming together in the centers were going to create a bulk problem. I tried several other design variations for the center of the blocks, but liked the black-and-white centers best. The final solution was to add black buttons in the centers of the plates. These hid the bulk, but also added interesting texture and focus.

Buttons in the center of the plates helped to hide fabric bulk.

Looking for a different direction for this quilt, I decided to use a blooming grid set. My original drawing had grid divisions of 12", 9", 6", and 3". Once the foundations were printed, I realized that the 12" blocks in the borders were much too large. So I revised the grid for 9" blocks in the border rather than following the true blooming grid (fig. 1).

One of my favorite design techniques is to use color to hide the block structure. In this case, I carried the lime green center background into the border blocks to give the illusion of curved lines and to blur the actual block edges.

I like to piece the backs of my quilts, with the back relating to the theme of the quilt. For DOTTIE DRESDEN, I used the Broken Dishes pattern and once again used all dotted fabrics (fig. 2). My label was computer generated and features even more dots (fig. 3).

Fig. 1. *The blooming grid was revised to include 9" blocks in the border.*

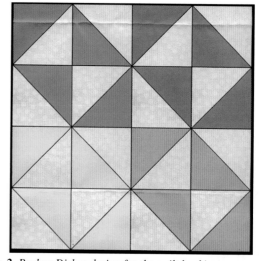

Fig. 2. *Broken Dishes design for the quilt backing*

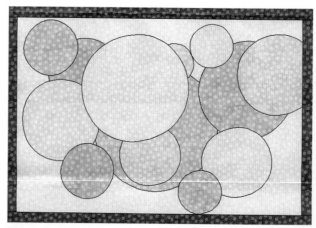

Fig. 3. *Computer-generated quilt label*

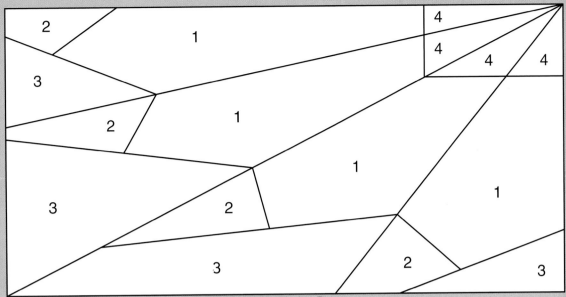

3" x 6" Paper-Piecing Pattern

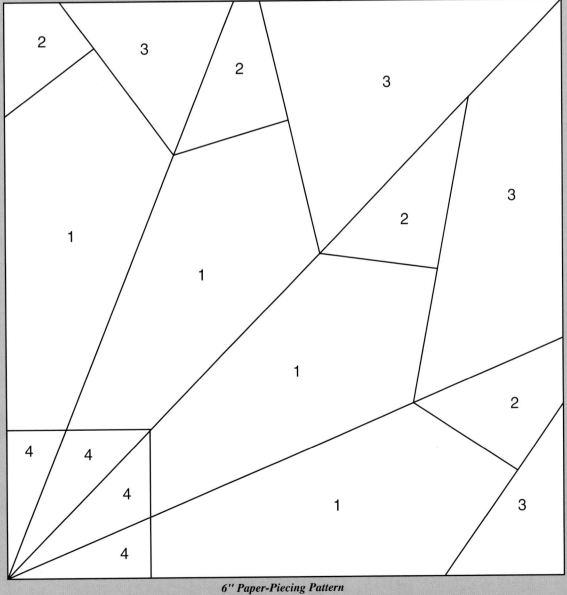

6" Paper-Piecing Pattern

Finalist

Nancy Stewart

Pitman, New Jersey

In a lively performance of *A Stitch in Time* at the school where I taught, a group that called themselves Seven Quilts for Seven Sisters presented its program that featured song, dance, history, stories, skits, and its quilts.

I found out that one of the sisters taught basic hand quilting. Because my goal was to learn to quilt upon retiring, I decided that 1996 was the year to begin my quilt journey.

Since retiring in 2000, I have become a serious quilter. I try to do something quilt related each day. Some days I spend as much as eight to ten hours quilting. My dear husband is most understanding, thank goodness.

After taking classes with Judith Thompson, who was the Best of Show winner in the 1997 American Quilter's Society Show and Contest, she has been the person who has influenced my work most. If it had not been for her confidence in me, I probably would not have entered this quilt to be judged.

I am not an artist or designer. I was a physical education teacher – how far from the artistic spectrum! Yet, I love color, fabric, and putting it all together in a quilt. I tend to use the Baltimore Album style in making my quilts and am smitten with appliqué quilts. Most of my quilts are done by hand. Of course, this takes considerably longer than using a machine so I do not finish many quilts within a year's time. Yet, after 32 years of a hectic career, it is relaxing to do hand work.

Inspiration and Design

In Judith Thompson's Dresden Plate class, I had no idea which direction I was headed with this quilt. The idea came to me to let the fabric be my guide. I began referring to the large plates as dinner plates because, to me, a Dresden Plate was made of fine china from Dresden, Germany.

The fabrics consist of nineteenth-century reproduction prints, contemporary, sateen, antique chintz, and small pieces from my 42-year-old wedding gown. I positioned a window template on the fabrics to obtain the desired petals for the plates.

Nancy's photo by Lifetouch Portrait Studios, Inc.

SOIRÉE AU JARDIN
56" x 69"

"SOIRÉE AU JARDIN means an elegant evening garden party. I think of the large plates as dinner plates, the small plates as dessert plates, and the border as the garden."

Fussy-cut hummingbirds

The trapunto in the sashing was stuffed from the back. I basted designer cloth around the design and stuffed it using a large needle. The sashing was stipple quilted to enhance the design.

The most challenging part of the construction was making the petals in the plates align as perfectly as possible. Otherwise, the design would have lost its desired effect. Each plate was made of a different fabric, which stimulates the viewer to study the quilt more carefully.

The most challenging part of quilting was the stipple quilting in the sashing because it was done by hand. I set goals for myself each day to complete a specific amount, but I think they were too high because I never met them. I will think twice before committing to that much hand stipple quilting again.

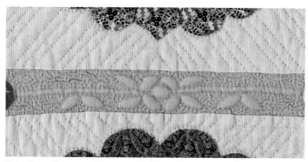
Stipple quilting and trapunto in the sashing

The flowers I enjoy in my garden were my inspiration for the border. In the garden, there are twelve uninvited ladies (bugs). See if you can find them. I also place a butterfly somewhere in my quilts. In this quilt, she is eating dessert.

Butterfly

Pairing Fabrics and Traditional Blocks

The large plate patterns came from several traditional designs. The fabrics determined the design of the plate. In several cases, the centers of the plates were made larger due to the fabric design. It is important to let your fabric talk to you. The following are the different designs that were used in this quilt (refer to photo on page 81):

Blocks 1, 3, 10, and 12 – Friendship Circle
The plate was rotated to position the point at twelve, three, six, and nine o'clock.

Block 2 – Friendship Circle
The template was used, with a concave pattern used for 20 petals.

Blocks 4 and 6 – Friendship Ring
The point petal was replaced with a rounded petal.

Blocks 7 and 9 – China Aster

Block 11 – Friendship Circle
The fabric determined the top of the petal.

The petals were marked on the wrong side of the fabric and hand stitched. I used freezer paper on the top of the petal, basted, and then appliquéd the plate to the background. Block 11 was needle-turn appliquéd. The two off-white flowers from my wedding gown were lined and stuffed so as not to see the seam line. I did not quilt either of these flowers because I was fearful that the material would not be able to take the needle.

Jane K. Wells

Fort Wayne, Indiana

A good friend, who has shared the joy of basket weaving and stained glass making with me, talked me into taking a quiltmaking class five years ago. My greatest protest was that I didn't want a bunch of fabric cluttering up my house as it had a few years earlier when I made my children's clothing and stuffed animals.

Anyway, I was immediately hooked and quilting has become a consuming force in my life. Never before have I been able to express my creativity and become so energized in any one endeavor. I feel such a sense of accomplishment at every step of my quiltmaking. I love attending quilt shows, have taken several classes, and have watched every episode of *Simply Quilts*.

My husband and I ran an exotic animal farm together and always shared a love of nature and the outdoors. I am a nurturer: three kids, many indoor and outdoor pets, plants everywhere, and now quilts. I usually incorporate this trait in my designs. When my husband died in an accident last year, I felt life was bleak. My sister encouraged me to become a team teacher at a local quilt shop, and that has helped bring me alive again.

I love sharing with our students and inspiring them to tap into their own creativity. Quilters are some of the nicest people you'll ever meet. Subsequently, my sister and I have also formed a quilt pattern design business called Crafty Ol' Broads.

Inspiration and Design

My son was a Peace Corps volunteer in Guatemala, and when visiting that country, I fell in love with the beautiful hand-woven striped fabrics. I had just seen a demonstration on making the Dresden Plate and was itching to try it.

Wanting to make a large, graphic wallhanging, I decided to use the Guatemalan fabric for the Dresden Plate flowers, and make a background of intense colors representing a colorful sky. Somehow, the flowers developed an attitude of their own, much like my garden flowers, and the main large flower became the mother plant, spilling out vines of babies.

The vine flowing from the large flower leads the eye around to all the smaller flowers.

GUATEMALAN WILDFLOWERS
55" x 73"

"My favorite part of quilting is designing, but I also love playing with color and fabric and actually putting the pieces together."

My favorite quilting tool is my design wall. I design quilts each night as I sleep, and then they evolve on this wall. What fun! Wanting GUATEMALAN WILDFLOWERS to make a bold, graphic statement, I liked the idea of a second design in the background.

At first, the background was going to be diamond shapes in ascending layers of colors and sizes. However, in playing around on my design wall, I liked the look of blending the colors through half-square triangles better. The block size was determined by the fact that I didn't want my Dresden Plates too small because the Guatemalan fabric needed a little size to show itself off.

Creating a Wildflower Garden

For all of the larger flowers, I used a 22½-degree wedge template; hence 16 wedges were sewn together to make one plate. For the smaller flowers, I cut strips of fabric, stacked them, and used a wedge ruler to cut the petals. Because the background is symmetrical, I felt the flowers were better off asymmetrical as most wildflowers and my gardens are.

The ending wedges of the flowers that form a partial Dresden Plate were caught in the block seam allowances. All the flowers and vines were pinned in place. I used invisible thread and a blind-hem stitch to machine appliqué the flowers, turning the center under about ¼".

Most vines were made using 1¼" wide fabric cut on the bias, I stitched a slight ¼" seam, inserted the ⅜" bias bar, and pressed the seam to one side in the back of the stem. A few of the vines that twirl at the ends were made using 1" wide bias fabric folded over a ¼" bias bar. I used spray starch and pressed with a hot iron as curves were coaxed into the vines. Notice that the vines travel in and out of each flower, all eventually tracing back to the mother flower. Often, the vines actually begin and end hidden on the underside of the flowers.

Two green fabrics were stitched together for the leaves. Once the seam allowance was pressed open, leaf shapes that I had freehand cut from freezer paper were pressed onto the back of the stitched fabric. Then, about ¼" was cut around each leaf and liquid starch was used to press the cut edge over the pattern. After it dried, I gently peeled the pattern off, re-pressed, and pinned leaves onto the vine. Invisible thread and a blind-hem stitch were used to apply the vines and leaves.

I heavily quilted all the background but mostly stitched in the ditch on the flowers. This gave a lovely texture to the whole quilt and made the flowers and vines pop!

Heavy quilting in the background gives focus to the flowers and vines.

Dresden
PLATE
PATTERNS

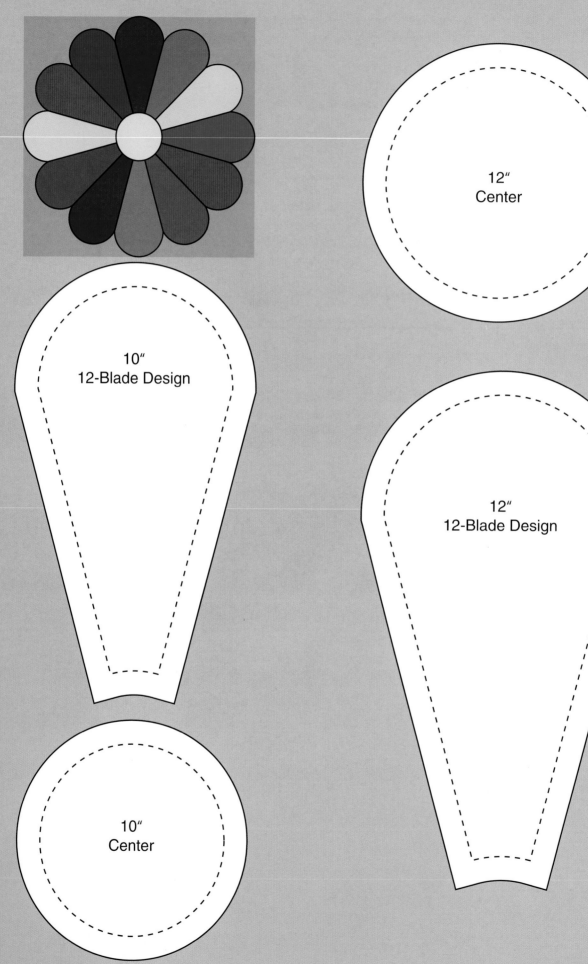

12″
Center

10″
12-Blade Design

12″
12-Blade Design

10″
Center

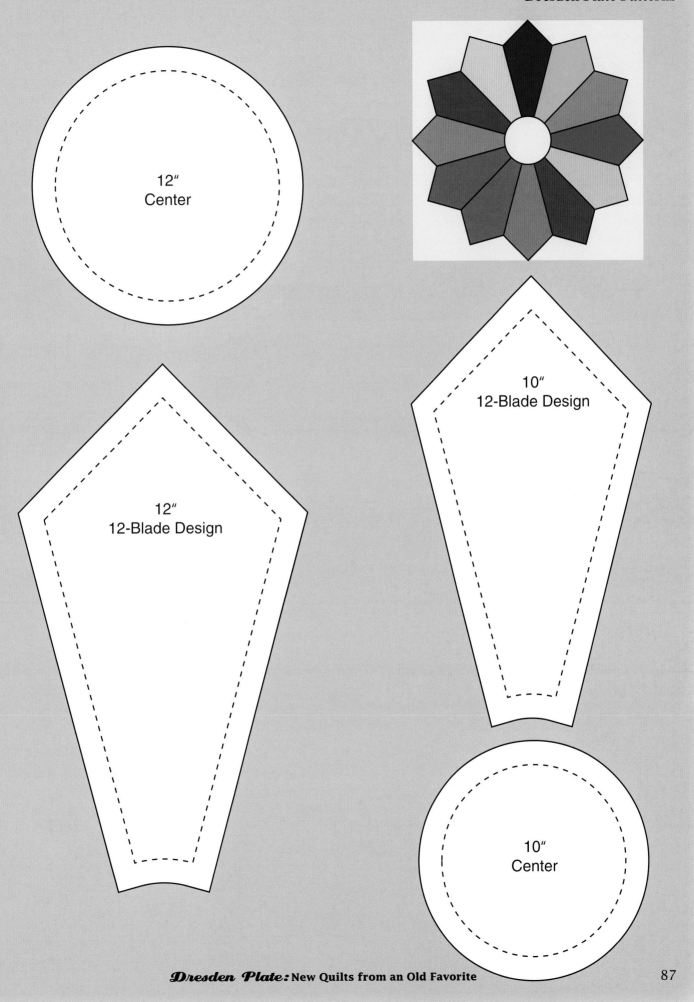

12″
Center

12″
12-Blade Design

10″
12-Blade Design

10″
Center

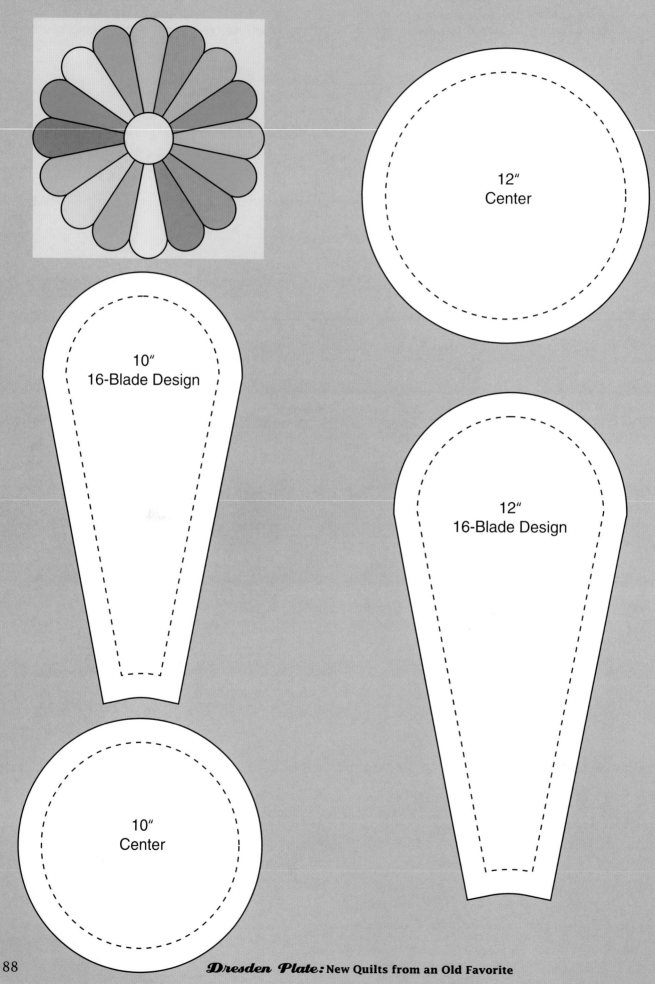

12"
Center

10"
16-Blade Design

12"
16-Blade Design

10"
Center

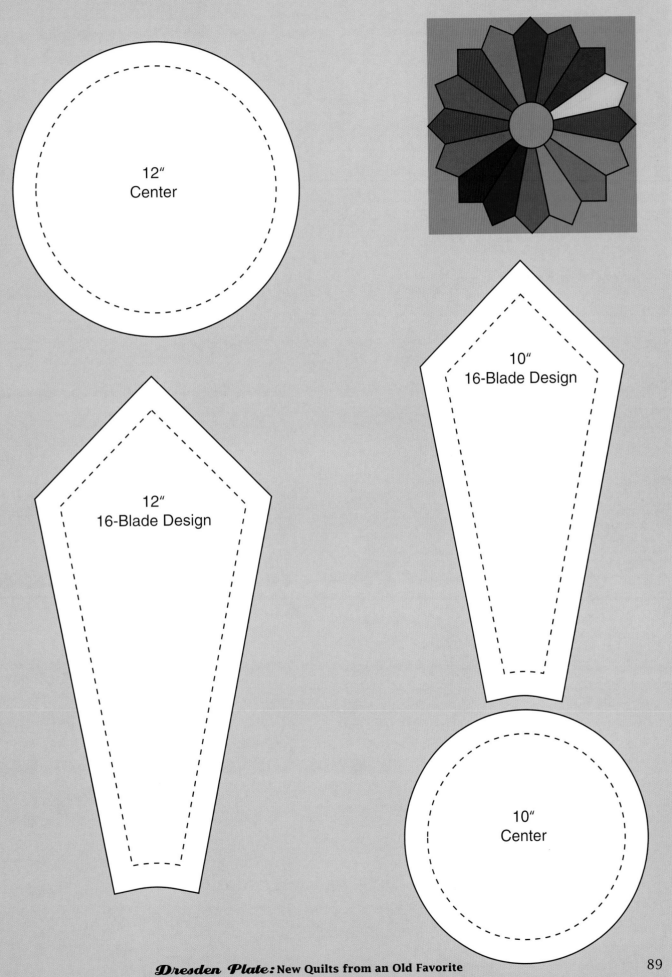

12″
Center

10″
16-Blade Design

12″
16-Blade Design

10″
Center

Dresden Plate Patterns

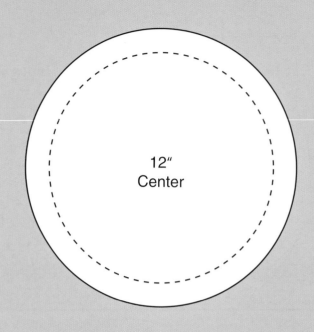

12″
Center

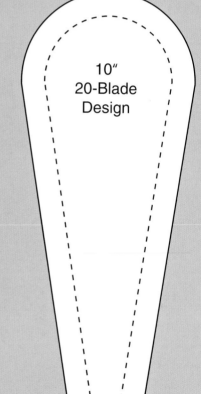

10″
20-Blade
Design

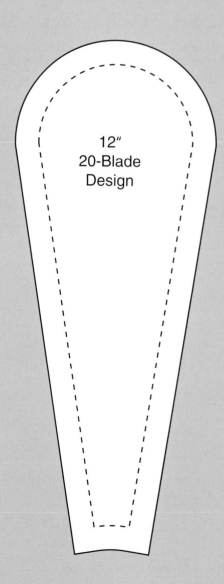

12″
20-Blade
Design

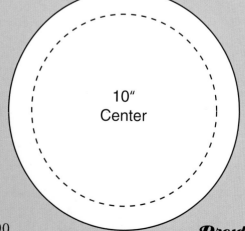

10″
Center

Dresden Plate: **New Quilts from an Old Favorite**

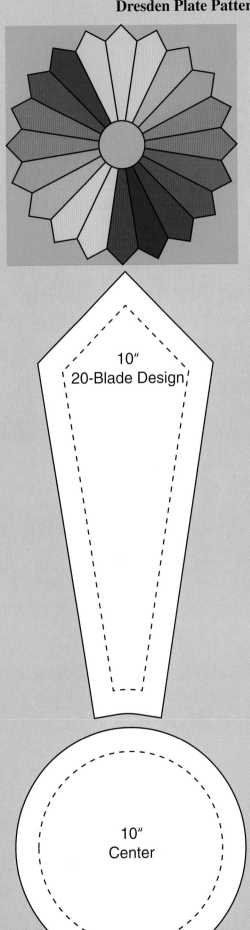

12″
Center

10″
20-Blade Design

12″
20-Blade Design

10″
Center

The Museum of the American

is truly an exhilarating place to learn more

MAQS is the world's largest and foremost museum devoted to quilts and the only museum dedicated to today's quilts and quiltmakers. Established in 1991 by AQS founders Bill and Meredith Schroeder as a not-for-profit organization, MAQS is located in a 27,000 square-foot facility. It was designed specifically to display quilts effectively and safely. Three expansive galleries envelope visitors in color, exquisite stitchery, and design.

The highlight of any visit is The William & Meredith Schroeder Gallery, which displays a rotating installation of quilts from the museum's permanent collection of over 200 quilts. Before MAQS opened, the Schroeders had acquired a private collection of remarkable quilts. In addition to being a source of wonder for the collectors, the collection came to recognize extraordinary contemporary quilts and their makers. Through the Schroeder's generosity, the nucleus of the museum collection was formed. In addition, the permanent collection includes award-winning quilts from the annual Quilt Show and Contest. Educational programs offered

in three well-equipped classrooms serve local and national audiences. Specifically, MAQS offers an annual schedule of in-depth workshops taught by master quilters. Children and families can participate in hands-on projects. Exhibitions developed by MAQS, like New Quilts from an Old Favorite, travel to other galleries and museums, helping educate and inspire a wider spectrum of viewers. The

photo by Jessica Byassee

Quilter's Society (MAQS)...

about quilts, quiltmaking, and quilters

MAQS shop and bookstore offer very special quilt-related merchandise as well as fine crafts by artisans from this region and beyond. One of the largest selections of quilt books anywhere can be found in the shop.

Located in historic downtown Paducah, Kentucky, MAQS is open year-round 10 A.M. to 5 P.M., Monday through Saturday. From April 1 through October 31, it is also open Sundays from 1 to 5 P.M. The entire facility is wheelchair accessible.

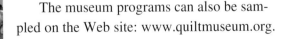

The museum programs can also be sampled on the Web site: www.quiltmuseum.org.

For more information,
e-mail: info@quiltmuseum.org
call: (270) 442-8856
or write: MAQS
PO Box 1540
Paducah, KY 42002-1540

Other AQS Books

This is only a small selection of the books available from the American Quilter's Society. AQS books are known worldwide for timely topics, clear writing, beautiful color photos, and accurate illustrations and patterns. The following books are available from your local bookseller, quilt shop, or public library.

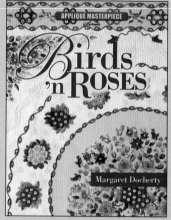

#7013   us$24.95

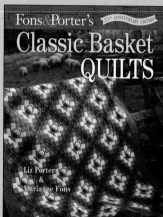

#7011   us$22.95

#7010   us$21.95

#6897   us$22.95

#6677   us$21.95

#6905   us$24.95

#6896   us$22.95

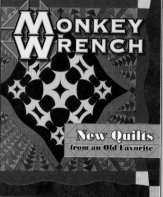

#6412   us$21.95

#5883   us$24.95

LOOK for these books nationally.
CALL or **VISIT** our Web site at

1-800-626-5420

www.AmericanQuilter.com